P9-CDX-885

CURE FOR THE COMMON LIFE
Small Group Study

Based on Cure for the Common Life by Max Lucado

Prepared by People Management International, Inc.

THOMAS NELSON
Since 1798

NASHVILLE   DALLAS   MEXICO CITY   RIO DE JANEIRO

© 2006 Max Lucado

All rights reserved. No portion of this book may be reproduced, stored in a retrieval system, or transmitted in any form or by any means—electronic, mechanical, photocopy, recording, or any other—except for brief quotation in printed reviews, without the prior permission of the publisher.

Published in Nashville, Tennessee, by Thomas Nelson. Thomas Nelson is a registered trademark of Thomas Nelson, Inc.

Thomas Nelson, Inc., titles may be purchased in bulk for educational, business, fund-raising, or sales promotional use. For information, please e-mail SpecialMarkets@ThomasNelson.com.

This small group study is an extension of *Cure for the Common Life* by Max Lucado. As such, it is a merger of Max Lucado's expressions with the technology expressions of the System for Identifying Motivated Abilities (SIMA®). Copyright in Max Lucado, subject to expressions based on or related to SIMA®, copyright People Management International, Inc.

Compiled and written by William Hendricks and Richard Wellock for People Management International, Inc.

This book contains significant copyrighted materials in the exploration of your design. S.T.O.R.Y. is a derivative of SIMA® (System for Identifying Motivated Abilities). SIMA® is registered and copyrighted by People Management International, Inc., P.O. Box 1004, Avon, CT 06001-1004.

Scripture quotations, unless otherwise noted, are taken from the HOLY BIBLE, NEW INTERNATIONAL VERSION. Copyright © 1973, 1978, 1984 International Bible Society. Used by permission of Zondervan. All rights reserved.

ISBN: 978-1-41850-605-6

Printed in the United States of America

HB 12.16.2020

Contents

INTRODUCTION
FINDING YOUR SWEET SPOT

In his book *Cure for the Common Life*, Max Lucado urges readers to find their "sweet spots" in life. Ever heard of a sweet spot? It refers to place on a golf club (or baseball bat or tennis racket) where you get the most power and control out of your swing. Hit a ball in the sweet spot and you can send it flying forever. So much energy for so little effort!

People have sweet spots, too. God has designed all human beings to do certain things well and in a way that is totally natural to them. For instance, one person has a knack for numbers. Another is a great problem-solver. Someone else has a nose for a bargain. Yet another is a creative genius. Every person has a sweet spot. And life makes sense when you find your spot and keep "hitting the ball" there.

So how do you find your own sweet spot? As Max describes in *Cure for the Common Life*, each of us has moments in our lives when, seemingly by accident, we hit a home run. Just knock it right out of the park to everyone's amazement. These moments are not accidents. It's not just a coincidence. There's a reason you wrote the best paper in your class in junior high school. There's a reason that you saved the day on the family vacation by knowing how to get your dad's stalled car re-started in a driving rainstorm. It wasn't just a rookie coincidence that enabled you to make a key observation that helped your boss save face with his superior.

When it comes to sweet spots there are no accidents, only incidents. They are moments when you're "in the zone." Situations in which the way God made you lines up with what is needed at the time. When that happens— wham! You hit the ball in your sweet spot and there it goes! To you it may not seem like a big deal, but to someone who doesn't have the gifts you have, your natural response can seem like a feat of genius.

And here we come to an irony. Your sweet spot—your *giftedness*—is so natural and so instinctive that when you're using it, you don't even think about using it. You just use it. You wouldn't think of doing things any other way. Therefore, your giftedness may not seem remarkable to you. It's just you being you. For that reason, most of us have a hard time recognizing our sweet spots for what they are.

That's a problem, because if you don't know what your sweet spot is, you're going to have a hard time hitting the ball there. Oh, occasionally you'll connect. As they say, even a blind squirrel finds a nut now and then. But God doesn't want you to live in your sweet spot now and then. He wants you there most of the time.

When we use the term *giftedness* in this small group study, we are referring to the unique way in which an individual functions. *Giftedness* is a person's inborn core strengths and natural motivation, which he instinctively uses to do things that are satisfying and productive. Giftedness is not just what the person can do, but what he was *born* to do, enjoys doing, and does very well. Giftedness is more than talent or ability. Giftedness involves *motivation*—an inner drive or energy that compels an individual to do a certain thing.

Every human being has giftedness. Every single one. No matter what the level of his intelligence is. No matter what her DNA makeup is. No matter how damaged, disabled, dysfunctional, or compromised she may be. Every human is born with her own unique giftedness. Many people hear the term "gifted" and they think of spectacular performers: Michael Jordan, Oprah Winfrey, Bill Gates, Albert Einstein, Mother Teresa. Impressive people like that have giftedness, to be sure. But so do you. Giftedness is not about the spectacular, the amazing, or the one-of-a-kind. Giftedness is about who people are—their *personhood*.

Every human being has personhood. Your personhood is given to you by God. Your personhood fits you for particular tasks. Sometimes a person fits a task so well that unusual results occur—maybe even spectacular results. Like seven NBA championships. Or billions of dollars in wealth. Or a change in the way a society sees a minority group. Or a new theory, called "relativity." We rightfully celebrate spectacular results like those. But giftedness is not in the results; it's in the person. And every person does something naturally and instinctively that yields some worthy result. That activity—that innate ability and the motivation to use it—is what we call a person's giftedness.

In many schools today, some students are designated as "talented and gifted" students. That means they possess a heightened capacity for learning and require an enriched curriculum to stimulate their education. It's wonderful that experts have identified the needs of those students. However, when we use the term *giftedness* in this small group study, we are not referring to "talented and gifted" people. We are referring to *all* people. Everyone has her own giftedness, quite apart from how she learns.

God endows every person with a means to glorify him in very practical, evident ways. That is his gift to us. He allows us to enjoy the exercise of our gifts, so that we'll do them again and again. But the purpose of the gifts is twofold: to bring God glory and to do the things that he wants done in the world.

If you have such a hard time recognizing your sweet spot, how will you ever find out what it is? As usual, God has an answer for that: other people. Other people are like a mirror for your giftedness.

You live inside your skin and usually instinctively do what you were designed to do. You don't see your giftedness at work, but the rest of us do. "Wow, how did you do that?" we'll ask after you've penned the neatly crafted letter, or negotiated the bargain of the day at the yard sale, or made the blockbuster insight at the Bible study, or baked the to-die-for chocolate cake.

When someone remarks on something you've done and asks, "How did you do that?" they are celebrating your sweet spot. Pay attention to that! That is not just flattery. Whether they realize it or not, they are praising God, because God made you to do the thing that you do. So by highlighting your accomplishment and saying, "That's something," they are in effect telling God, "Way to go, God! Thank you for giving my friend here the ability to do what she does. That's something!"

Surprisingly, Max's advice to "do the most what you do the best" is hard to swallow for many people. It sounds like common sense, and yet it is not practiced very widely. Consider four reasons why:

(1) **Many people don't know what they do best.** It's almost impossible to determine what you do best on your own. As a result, most people are only vaguely aware of what they do best. So how can they be intentional about something they don't even know about?

(2) **Many people minimize the importance of what they do best.** Your sweet spot is natural and instinctive. You don't have to "work" at doing what you do best. It comes naturally. For that reason, many people discount what they do

well and enjoy doing. "It's no big deal," they say. And if it's no big deal, then that means it's not very important—not important enough to spend most of one's time there, right? But of course your sweet spot *is* a big deal! It's a big deal to God, who gave you the gift. And it's a big deal to the rest of us, who need you to exercise your gift.

(3) Many people assume that it's wrong to enjoy what they do best. Functioning in your sweet spot is fun! There's joy and satisfaction attached to it. Unfortunately, many people think that if something is fun, it can't be worthwhile. To them, fun is play, not work. They'll even say, "Why do you think they call it 'work'?" But God gives us joy in what we do best so that we'll do it over and over—gladly! He wants us to do what he designed us to do best.

(4) Many people assume that "getting" to do what you do best is a luxury. Many a career has been derailed because people knowingly chose paths that did not fit them. They mistakenly believed that only after one has succeeded do they get to do what they *want* to do. Success comes from concentrating on our strengths—doing the most what we do the best. If that feels like a luxury, then let us live in luxury! After all, God gave us work as a gift (Eccl. 3:12–13; 5:19). Sin made work into drudgery and toil. Don't cooperate with sin by hating your job. Do something you love, to the glory of God.

Does God really want us to do the most what we do the best? Yes! Each of us has been given unique gifts for making our own individual contribution to the world. So what happens if we rarely or never use our gifts? Clearly, we won't make the contribution God intended us to make. In that case, we are resisting God. That can't help but displease his heart. And in a way, not using our gift is an insult to him. In effect we are saying, "God, I'm not going to unwrap the gift you gave me. I'm not going to experience the joy you wanted me to have when using it. And I'm not going to benefit anyone else. Instead, I'm going to spend my time doing things you haven't gifted me to do. I may end up unhappy, and I may be unproductive, but that seems like what I'd like to do. So thanks, but no thanks, for the gift you gave me."

That's not what you want to tell God, is it? If not, make the effort to identify your sweet spot—what you do best. Then wrap your life around that. Do the most what you do the best!

In fact, Max himself found his sweet spot only when someone else helped him to see it.

"But isn't Max's sweet spot a bit obvious?" you may be thinking. "He's one of the best teachers I've ever heard!" You may recognize that about Max, but it wasn't obvious to him. As he describes the situation in *Cure for the Common Life*, at one point in his ministry, Max was burning out. At the time, his church was bursting at the seams. After a lot of prayer and planning, the church decided it needed a new building on some new property. So they raised the money. They bought the land. They built the building. They rejoiced in God's faithfulness. By all rights, Max should have been thrilled.

But he wasn't. He was straining. He was going through the motions. He was doing all the "right" things that he thought a pastor is "supposed" to do. But he wasn't taking joy in it. That lack of joy was a sure sign that Max was out of his sweet spot. Mind you, he was doing good things. But he wasn't doing the best thing for the way God had designed him. If anything, Max came to feel at times as if he was doing the most what he does the worst!

Here's the irony: Max didn't know that. He didn't know his sweet spot.

Maybe it was obvious to everyone else, but it wasn't obvious to him. As a result, he ended up feeling like a machine, not a person. He seriously began to wonder whether he was cut out for the pastorate.

Soon, God brought someone into Max's path to help him with his predicament. Rick Wellock, an executive coach and organizational consultant with People Management International, Inc. (PMI), spent a day with Max, taking him through the process described in *Cure for the Common Life*—quite similar to the process this small group study will take you through. Rick took Max back to moments in his life when he was doing things he loved doing and felt he did well. In other words, he took Max back to the moments he was living in his sweet spot. Here are a few of those experiences:

> *Max told Rick about elementary school, when he read every biography in the library.*
>
> *As a high-school freshman, delivering an election-winning speech.*
>
> *In a literature course, where he wrote and rewrote short stories by the hour.*
>
> *The first time he ever gave a Bible lesson. It was to a group of middle-schoolers. To Max's amazement, they listened!*
>
> *How he developed a process for preparing his sermons.*

Rick spent a couple of hours interviewing Max about stories like these, where satisfaction and success intersected in his life.

Later, Max received a lengthy report that went into great detail about all the things that are a part of his sweet spot. After talking with Rick more, Max discovered the ways that God had designed him. That discovery was a breakthrough in Max's life and ministry. When he finally realized what God made his heart leap up to do, he felt like a new man. He felt free. He was able to see why his eyes had glazed over during committee meetings spent picking out paint colors, poring over budgets, debating the number of stalls needed in the bathrooms. Those were important matters, but Max realized that those things belonged to someone else's sweet spot, not his.

As a result, Max redefined his role in the church. He stopped doing tasks that didn't fall in his sweet spot, and stuck to the tasks that had his name on them. Result: Max started hitting a lot more home runs.

<u>We should pay attention when someone praises our sweet spot</u>. That person is celebrating what we do best, and we should take note of that affirmation. It's telling us an important truth about how God has made us.

But sometimes people tell us about how God has made us in a very different way. Unfortunately, they package the truth about us in a negative label. For instance, imagine someone who has organized a meeting down to the last detail. Every minute has been carefully scheduled. Everything in the room has been painstakingly arranged. Every person in the meeting has been given a set of neat, orderly notes ahead of time. Then a coworker comes in and tells the person who pulled all of that together, "My, aren't you the perfectionist!"

Is that a true statement about the person? Is she, in fact, a "perfectionist"? Well, perhaps. That may actually be quite accurate. She may love to get things right. Indeed, she may love to get things perfect. But what's wrong with the label "perfectionist"? It's a negative label. There's a sense of shame attached to it, as if there's something wrong with aiming at perfection. So is it helpful to call that person a perfectionist? No, it actually ends up shaming her for doing what she does best.

For every kind of sweet spot, there's a negative, shame-based label: perfectionist, know-it-all, glory-hound, drama queen, dreamer, over-achiever, cowboy, scrooge, egghead, spoil-sport, one-trick pony, dweeb, geek, jack-of-all-trades and master-of-none. The list is endless. It's a sad list, no? Labels like these express the truth about someone's sweet spot, but in a terribly destructive way.

We <u>need to be on our guard against negative labels</u>. First, we need to watch out when others label us in a shaming way. We need to correct their misstatement, even if only in our head. So if they call us a perfectionist, we need to say to ourselves, "Well, yes, I guess I do aim at perfection. That's part of my sweet spot. I'll own that motivation to get things right. That's how God made me. I'll celebrate it. I won't be ashamed of my sweet spot."

We also need to resist labeling others. Yes, sometimes their sweet spot can seem a bit humorous to us. Sometimes it may even annoy us. But that's only because others are unlike us. That doesn't make them bad people; it only makes them different people. If we have to point out that difference, let us do it in a positive way (parents especially should pay attention to this). For instance: "Sharon, I'm so glad you handled the set-up for this meeting. If it had been left up to me, things would have been completely disorganized. But you've just done a perfect job putting everything together. I admire that! Thank you for doing what you do best."

Ephesians 4:25 (NIV) tells Christians to speak the truth to one another, because we all belong to the same body. Verse 29 urges us to speak that truth in a way that builds others up. Our objective, the verse says, is to "benefit those that listen." By praising one another's sweet spots, using positive affirmation rather than negative labels, we give grace to each other and build up the body of Christ.

Would you like to do that? We at PMI know you would. That's why Max partnered with us to put together this small group study. Please understand that this guide can't duplicate the in-depth process that Max went through. He had a trained, experienced person interview him on his stories. He had an expert go over the transcript of those stories to identify the details of his giftedness. He had a seasoned coach help him gain a comprehensive understanding of his sweet spot, and he had the benefit of that coach's guidance to help him apply what he learned to countless areas of his life and ministry.

This small group study can't duplicate that sort of professional consultation, but you will still benefit enormously by going through this process. Our hope is that:

- You will see a pattern to how you function. You'll see that your sweet spot is something you come back to and repeat over and over.

- You will have some of your core strengths affirmed. Are you tired of being told about your weaknesses and what you do wrong? This process will show you what you do right!

- You will see that God has been involved in your whole life, even from your earliest years. Giftedness is inborn. God gave you yours in the womb. You'll see that your giftedness began showing up from your first day on earth.

- You will see that you are unique. Sure, you share some things in common with others. But no one is exactly like you. You will begin to discover what makes you unique from everyone else.

- You will see that your "wiring" has a lot of practical bearing on your life, including your career, marriage, parenting, relationships, etc.

- You will discover that things you don't like to do and don't do well are actually sweet spots for someone else. That means you don't have to do everything! Others can benefit *you* by contributing what *they* do best.

- You're going to discover some amazing gifts in the other people. By seeing them in their sweet spots, you will come to appreciate them in ways you never imagined.

There's one important key to getting the most out of this group: *follow the process.* It's really rather simple: Each time this group meets, you will tell sweet spot stories from your life and look for patterns. That sounds easy enough, right? In fact, for some it will sound too easy. But trust the process. It has a long track record of giving people insight into the core of their giftedness.

If you've ever tried to hit a golf ball, you'll understand what we mean by trusting the process. Golf looks like a simple enough activity. You put a little white ball on some grass, swing a club, and knock the ball a few hundred yards down the fairway, right? Except that's not what happens the first time you play golf. You discover that what Tiger Woods makes look simple is not so simple after all.

So do you just give up? No! You find someone to show you how to hold the club, connect with the ball, and improve your swing. Then you hit a lot of balls. At first you feel a little awkward, but if you stick with it you eventually will connect solidly with the ball.

The same is true for telling stories and looking for patterns. Work the process. Do what this study tells you to do. At first you may feel a little awkward, and it may not seem like you're "getting" it. Don't worry. The process works if you'll work the process. Max is confident of that. He's done it. God used it to change his life. And God can do the same for you.

FAQ

Q: Wouldn't it be easier to take a personality test or something to find out more about myself?

A: Personality tests, psychological inventories, and similar tools have their value. But the approach offered in this small group study is significantly different. For one thing, inventories and questionnaires ask *you* to evaluate your behavior, which is inherently subjective. In this group, you'll tell about things you have actually done in the real world, which is much more objective. Another difference is that tests and inventories compare you to other people, placing you in a category or labeling you as a "type" of person. That won't happen here. We're interested in what makes you *unique*. Yet a third difference is that filling out a questionnaire may or may not be interesting to you. In this process, you're going to have a lot of fun!

Session One
WHAT'S YOUR STORY?

Getting Started

Welcome to *Cure for the Common Life Small Group Study*, based on the book by Max Lucado. In these sessions, our aim is to discover the unique ways in which God has designed each of us, and then learn to follow our design as we live each day. We're going to go beyond mere information to *transformation*—actually living differently as a result of going through these sessions together.

But first, let's state the obvious. Each of us comes into this first session from a very different place—literally. Some of us came here from work, some from home. Some of us are feeling happy, and some of us are feeling distressed or tired. We all bring a different mindset to the group today. So, as instructed in the following activity, take a moment to tell the person next to you what sort of day you've had so far, and what's on your mind as you come to this discussion group. Then allow the other person to share.

Sharing and Listening Activity 1

1. **Person 1:** Briefly tell the person next to you (Person 2) what sort of day you've had so far. Where have you focused your energy today before coming to the group?

2. **Person 2:** Briefly describe what you heard Person 1 say.

When Person 1 is finished, turn the conversation around.
Person 2 should now respond to (1) above.

Paying Attention

To a casual observer, the things we just told each other may seem common-place. But the whole premise of this group is that what seems ordinary is in fact extraordinary *if we pay attention to it*. The key is to pay attention. That's what we're going to do in the next few sessions—learn to pay attention. Our design—our *giftedness*—is "hidden in plain sight." We use this giftedness all the time, every day. But we don't always notice it. It's so natural that we think nothing of it. This group is going to help us to start paying attention to our giftedness, and to see it in action.

In the next activity, go back to the person you just spoke with about your day. This time, tell her about an activity you really enjoy doing, something that gives you a great deal of satisfaction. It could be almost anything: baking a pie, working in the yard, watching a hockey game, playing with your kids or grandkids, talking on the phone with a friend, reading a good book. It doesn't matter what the activity is. Just make sure it's an activity you enjoy doing. Describe what that activity is and why you enjoy it so much.

What Do We Mean by Satisfaction?

One way to identify a sweet spot area is that the activity you are doing feels satisfying. That is, it is satisfying because you enjoy doing it. You get something back from doing it—a sort of "emotional payoff," if you will—and it feels great. The activity just makes sense to you. It is worth doing. You feel a sense of meaning and purpose to it, and when you do it, you feel energized. Indeed, you feel joyful. Your heart leaps up. You'd be happy to do it again. You're excited and enthusiastic.

All of these reactions, of course, are subjective. And that's the tricky thing about satisfaction: it means different things to different people. Only you know what feels satisfying to you.

For one person, satisfaction means the sense of completion and a job well done when she finally reaches a goal. For another person satisfaction comes from seeing light spring up in a person's eyes as he finally understands what she has been explaining. For someone else, satisfaction is the thrill of winning a competition. For still another, satisfaction is the feeling of contentment and "rightness" that comes when he sees a carefully laid plan work out.

God has given each of us a desire for some particular outcome. That desire drives our behavior. It lies at the center of our sweet spot. In fact, it's what draws us to the sweet spot. That desire makes the sweet spot sweet. We do the things we do because we are looking to satisfy our core, God-given desire. And when we fulfill that desire, we feel a sense of contentment. Our desire has been satisfied. That's the way giftedness works.

So does that mean that anything that gives us pleasure or satisfaction is part of our sweet spot? Not necessarily. Giftedness is not about satisfaction, it's about motivation. It's about using our God-given strengths to achieve an outcome that we are motivated to pursue. Satisfaction is an *end result* of doing what we are motivated and able to do. If all that mattered in life were our satisfaction, we would get into lots of trouble, because there are numerous ways to gain pleasure and satisfaction without using giftedness. Some people would be quite content eating a box of chocolates. Others would be happy to watch television all day. Neither of those activities takes giftedness!

We humans can derive a great deal of satisfaction and enjoyment from using our giftedness, but that's not why God gave us our gifts. According to Ephesians 2:10, God gave us our gifts to do "good works" that he wanted done in the world. That's the *purpose* of giftedness—to serve him and make a contribution to others. The satisfaction that we feel when we make that contribution is a bonus.

And a wonderful bonus it is! By allowing us to enjoy what we do best, the Lord has ensured that we'll seek to do that best thing again and again. That's the nature of giftedness.

Sharing and Listening Activity 2

1. **Person 1:** Tell the person next to you about an activity you enjoy doing and find satisfying. Give an example to illustrate what you're talking about.

Hint: Pick an activity in which you actually *do* something, rather than just experience something. For instance, you may enjoy driving through the countryside in the fall to take in the vivid colors of the foliage. But that's more of an experience than an achievement. However, if you planned and made a special lunch to take along on such a trip, and you enjoyed doing that, then talk about that. The point is, pick an activity that lets your partner hear about you *doing* something.

2. Describe the satisfaction you gain from that activity. Be as specific as you can. Don't just say, "I like it." What do you like about it? What is it about that activity that feels so satisfying?

When Person 1 is finished, turn the conversation around. Person 2 should now respond to (1) and (2) above.

Motivate Me!

We can already see that there are differences in what motivates each one of us. We enjoy different activities because God made each of us so differently. What would happen if each of us spent most of our time in positive activities that captured our interest and energy? We'd be highly motivated, productive people.

In the next activity, go back to the person next to you once again, and this time tell him about a time in your past when you did an activity you enjoyed doing and feel you did well. Maybe it was a science project in junior high school or saving up

What's the Satisfaction?

Examples:
- A job well done.
- Finally getting it finished.
- Feeling like I've made a difference.
- Solving the problem.
- Doing my best.
- Getting a good deal.
- Being equal to the challenge.
- Meeting a real need someone had.

for a new bike. Maybe it was a poem you memorized or a role you played in a church Christmas pageant. Maybe it was a surprise birthday party you planned for your spouse. Whatever you decide to talk about, the key is that you enjoyed doing the activity and that you felt satisfied with what you accomplished.

> Remember, God planned and packed you on purpose for his purpose.
> – Max Lucado

Things I Enjoyed Doing and Did Well

Examples:

- Collected bottle caps to earn a prize.

- Pitched a no-hitter in a little league baseball game.

- Organized my stamp collection.

- Learned to handle a canoe at summer camp.

- Took charge of our Scout troop when the Scout master got injured in a fall.

- Painted house numbers on curbs one summer and earned $3,500.

- Won a debate competition in high school.

- Fixed up an old motorcycle to ride.

- Oversaw publicity for our sorority and got a feature article written about one of our service projects.

- Landed my first "real" job by figuring out where the hiring manager ate breakfast and sitting down at his table to introduce myself.

- Negotiated the purchase of our first home.

- Came up with a plan for purchasing and installing a new computer system at work.

- Planned my dad's 60th birthday party. He said it was the best time he'd ever had.

- Made a scrapbook for my Sunday school class.

Sharing and Listening Activity 3

1. **Person 1:** Tell the person next to you about a time in your past when you did an activity you enjoyed and felt you did well. Describe what you did and how you went about doing it.

2. Describe the satisfaction you gained from that activity. Be specific. What was it about that activity that felt so satisfying?

When Person 1 is finished, turn the conversation around. Person 2 should now respond to (1) and (2) above.

FAQ

Q: What if I enjoy something that is wrong or is bad for me, such as an addiction or something the Bible tells me not to do?

A: Ironically, addictions and many sins are initially satisfying because they take advantage of the normal desires and motivations he has placed in our hearts. The desire itself is not wrong, but what we choose to satisfy the desire can be very wrong. What makes an activity sinful is not the motivation that gives rise to it or the satisfaction that comes from it, but the way in which it offers to satisfy our desires apart from God.

Reflecting

You've just told the person next to you about an activity that you currently enjoy doing, as well as about an activity that you enjoyed doing sometime in the past. Telling these stories and hearing about other people's stories have probably made you think of other activities you've enjoyed doing and feel you did well. Pay attention to those activities! The reason you enjoy them has something to do with how God has designed you.

To help you pay attention and to take note of your giftedness, please take a moment now to write down a brief description of the experiences you discussed and what you learned about yourself from those experiences on the next page. Then check with your neighbor to make sure that what you've written down adequately describes what he heard you say.

Reflections

Pulling It Together

As we finish Session One, it may seem like we haven't done very much—we've just been telling stories. But in fact, we've done something very important. We've tapped into the heart of your God-given design in just a tiny way. By telling about things you have enjoyed doing and feel you did well, you have allowed us to see you in your sweet spot. In the sessions to come, you'll tell more stories, and we'll get to see even more of your sweet spot, your giftedness.

In *Cure for the Common Life*, Max asks:

What have you always done well? And what have you always loved to do?

That last question trips up a lot of well-meaning folks. *God wouldn't let me do what I like to do—would he?* According to Paul, he would. "God is working in you to help you *want to do* and be *able to do* what pleases him" (Phil. 2:13 NCV). Your Designer couples the "want to" with the "be able to." Desire shares the driver's seat with ability. "Delight yourself in the Lord and he will give you the desires of your heart" (Ps. 37:4 NIV). Your Father is too gracious to assign you to a life of misery. As Thomas Aquinas wrote, "Human life would seem to consist in that which each man most delights, that for which he especially strives, and that which he particularly wishes to share with his friends." (page 28)

For the Next Lesson

1. This week, tell a trusted friend or loved one about the satisfying activities you described in this session. Be sure to describe what it is about those activities that feels so satisfying.

2. Using the guide provided here, make a list of activities you have done in your life that you enjoyed doing and feel you did well. Put as many items on the list as you like. The key is that you found the activities satisfying.

FAQ

Q: What if I can't think of any activities I've enjoyed doing?

A: Sometimes people do get stuck trying to remember things they've enjoyed doing. If that's the case for you, it's possible you may be trying too hard. That is, you may be be trying to think of activities you've just *loved* doing, or felt *passionate* about doing. But not everyone feels "passionate" often. That's okay. What are some simple activities that you favor? It could be something as uncomplicated as getting the kitchen sink clean, or crocheting, or balancing your checkbook. It doesn't matter whether other people think the activity is significant or satisfying. What is a satisfying activity for *you*?

Another possibility is that you've experienced a lot of pain in your life—for example, while growing up. In that case, you may remember only the pain, and not much else. That's understandable. But even though your circumstances were generally difficult, were there some activities you did that brightened your day or that you took pleasure in? Also, think of activities from more recent years.

As you try to come up with activities that you've enjoyed doing, consider things like hobbies, volunteer work, projects in school, extracurricular activities, things you did in the summer, activities at camp, vacations, trips you've taken, projects around the house, special relationships with people, or unusual opportunities that you've taken advantage of. The key is that the activity was something you *enjoyed* doing.

Lord, thank you for designing each one of us uniquely and for enabling us to catch just a glimpse of our uniqueness by paying attention to some moments when we were using our giftedness. Help us in the sessions to come to see much more clearly how you have made us, and what you have given us to work with. You have placed each of us here for a purpose, and you have fit us perfectly for that purpose. Help us to wake up to our design, so that we will find and follow your purpose for our lives.

Session Two
UNPACK YOUR LIFE

Getting Started

Welcome back. In *Cure for the Common Life*, Max points out that our design is not something we have to acquire, but something we already possess. We use it every day. Therefore, most of the time we're not even aware that we're using our design. We just use it. It's so natural to us that we don't think about it. As a result, it remains "hidden in plain sight." The purpose of this group is to help us pay attention to core strengths and motivation that we're already using instinctively. We are striving to discover our unique, God-given design, and then follow that design as we live each day.

We discover those things by telling stories about ourselves. Not just any stories, but stories that show us in our "sweet spot." We know we're in our sweet spot when

> You can't be your hero, your parent, or your big brother. You might imitate their golf swing or hair style, but you can't be them. You can only be you. All you have to give is what you've been given to give. Concentrate on who you are and what you have.
>
> – Max Lucado

we're doing an activity that we enjoy doing and feel we're doing well. At the end of the last session, we were asked to make a list of some of our "sweet spot activities." In the activity below, share with another person about one of those activities from your list. For this session, if possible, share with a different person than you talked with in Session One. If you did not make a list of your sweet spot activities, that's okay. Just go back to a time in your past and recall an activity that you enjoyed doing and feel you did well. As you did in the last session, follow the instructions below to tell the other person how you went about that activity, and what you found so satisfying about it. This session may feel repetitive to you, but don't give up! You will learn something about yourself from each experience that you share with your group.

What Was So Satisfying?

Examples:

- I liked the way it looked when I had finished the project. It just made me want to shout for joy!

- It was the thrill of finally figuring out what was wrong with the program. I mean, I wrestled and wrestled with it in my mind. Then suddenly, right in the middle of shaving, it was like, "I got it!" And I did. I'd figured it out.

- I realized that no one else was able to do what I could do. I was totally in a league of my own. That felt fantastic!

- I had worked and worked with her to learn those words and be able to read the sentences. She finally got it. And when she did, she looked up and smiled at me. That just brought tears to my eyes.

- I think it was that I had learned how to do it. You know, for the longest time everyone had said, "It can't be done. You'll never do it." But I put my mind to it, and, yeah, it was hard. But one day, I could do it. That was the satisfaction—just being able to show everyone I could do it.
- When I played the final note, just as it was dying out, the crowd went wild. They gave me a standing ovation. I just loved that response. They really seemed to appreciate what I had tried to give them.
- The fact that we got everything done on time and under budget was extremely satisfying. My plan worked!

Sharing and Listening Activity 1

1. Tell the person next to you about a time in your past when you did an activity that you enjoyed doing and feel you did well. Describe *what* you did and *how* you went about doing it. Do not go into *why* you did it. Just narrate what the other person would have seen you doing, as if a camcorder had been there to capture the action.

2. Describe the satisfaction you gained from the activity. Be specific. What was it about that activity that felt so satisfying?

Hint: Don't be afraid to "boast" a little bit in talking about the satisfaction. For example, if you performed on a stage and loved hearing the applause at the end, say that. If you competed in a contest and the satisfaction came from beating your opponent, say that. The satisfaction is what it is. Don't "edit" it just because it might make you look good. If you took pride in one of your accomplishments, own that!

When Person 1 is finished, turn the conversation around. Person 2 should now respond to (1) and (2) above.

Hint to the Listener:

Your objective is to encourage by listening. You can help the person telling the story by trying to picture her description in your mind. Ask her to fill in the picture by asking a question like, "What would I have seen you doing as you painted the picture/arranged the room/memorized your part in the play/led the meeting (or whatever she did)?" Try to get her to give you specific details.

Let the person tell her story. Don't get her off track by introducing your own experiences, as for instance: "You went hiking? Oh, I just love hiking! Did I ever tell you about the time my brother and I hiked the Appalachian Trail? It was two summers ago, and we really enjoyed getting out in the woods and . . . ." That's an interesting story—but tell it some other time. Right now, stay focused on the other person.

Reflecting

- Take a moment to write down in the space provided below what you found so satisfying in the activity you chose to tell about. (See "What Was the Satisfaction?" on the next page for examples.)

What Was the Satisfaction?

Examples:

- He said he liked the fact that he doubled his investment.
- For her it was just being part of a team—seeing her efforts join with other people's efforts.
- He loved being the go-to guy. He was the man with the plan.
- He kept trying to improve things and make them better.
- She said that running twenty-six miles was satisfying—that it was the greatest thing she'd ever done.
- I think she enjoyed making what she called the "perfect" soufflé.

- Take a moment to write down in the space provided some of the action words (or verbs) you used to accomplish your activity.

What Were the Action Words?

Examples:

- "I *organized* everybody."
- "I *set* goals and *made* a plan."
- "I *built* a working model of it first."
- "I just *thought* it up."
- "I *took* what I'd seen before and kind of *adapted* it for our use."
- "I *sold* them on the idea."
- "I *memorized* my lines."
- "I *wrote* up a report and then *delivered* it."

Okay, let's tell some more stories. As before, tell the person next to you about one of the sweet spot activities from your list. Or, if you don't have a list, go back to a time in your past and recall an activity that you enjoyed doing and feel you did well. Try to pick a story from a different period of your life than the last story. For example, if your last story was from childhood, try to pick a story from your teen or young adult years. If your last story was from adulthood, try to pick a story from your youth. Remember, the key is that you found the activity satisfying.

Sharing and Listening Activity 2

1. As before, tell the person next to you about a time in your past when you did an activity that you enjoyed doing and feel you did well. Describe what you did and how you went about doing it.

2. Describe the satisfaction you gained from the activity. Be specific. What was it about the activity that felt so satisfying?

When Person 1 is finished, turn the conversation around. Person 2 should now respond to (1) and (2) above.

Focusing

- Take a moment to write down in the space provided what you found so satisfying in the activity you just told about.

- Take a moment to write down in the space provided some of the action words (or verbs) you used to accomplish your activity.

Sharing and Listening Activity 3

Let's tell one more story in this session, using the same process. Tell the person next to you about one of the sweet spot activities from your list. Or, if you don't have a list, go back to a time in your past and recall an activity that you enjoyed doing and feel you did well.

1. As before, tell the person next to you about a time in your past when you did an activity that you enjoyed doing and feel you did well. Describe what you did and how you went about doing it.

2. Describe the satisfaction you gained from the activity. Be specific. What was it about the activity that felt so satisfying?

When Person 1 is finished, turn the conversation around. Person 2 should now respond to (1) and (2) above.

Discovering

- Take a moment to write down in the space provided what you found so satisfying in the activity you just told about.

- Take a moment to write down in the space provided some of the action words (or verbs) you used to accomplish your activity.

By listening to the person next to you tell his stories, you've now seen three snapshots of that person when he was in his sweet spot. Take a moment to tell the person next to you what you see him doing when he is in his sweet spot.

Hint: Stick to describing behaviors and keep your description straightforward. If all three stories shared were about the person solving a problem, say something like, "Your sweet spot seems to be about problem-solving. In all three stories you are solving a problem of some sort." Avoid generalities that cannot be tied to specific actions (even if they are true). For instance, don't say, "I see your stories as three examples of you serving the Lord."

Also avoid making judgments. Don't say, "You seem to enjoy meddling in other people's problems," or "You're kind of a perfectionist, aren't you?" Keep your description positive and affirming—always.

Pulling It Together

This brings us to the end of Session Two. For some of us, telling stories is a fun and interesting exercise, and we could easily keep going. For others, however, storytelling is not our "thing," and we may be wondering "What's the point?" Both reactions are legitimate, and both are driven by the way we're designed. The reason we're telling stories is that we're trying to discover how we naturally function by virtue of how God has designed us. If we pay attention to what we're actually doing when we're operating in our sweet spot, we'll discover our unique design—what we do best. And as we're going to see, figuring out what we do best will help us be much more effective in our practical, day-to-day lives.

For the Next Session

1. If you haven't already done so, make a list of activities you have done in your life that you enjoyed doing and feel you did well. Put as many items on the list as you like. The key is that you found the activities satisfying. (Use the guide provided on page 8).

2. Review the activities you talked about in Session 1 and Session 2.

   - Can you see any similarities between them?

   - Are there any common themes about the satisfaction you take from your sweet spot activities?

   - Are there any action words (verbs) that keep repeating in your stories?

3. Your design has significant implications for your everyday life. So think about the five areas of life listed below. Put a star (*) next to the area(s) where knowing your design could be the most helpful in your life. Perhaps it's the area in which you are currently experiencing the greatest frustrations.

   _____ Work

   _____ Marriage

   _____ Parenting

   _____ Relationships

   _____ Involvement in church

Lord, thank you for designing me uniquely. Psalm 139 says that you personally tailored me in the womb, like a craftsman weaving a beautiful tapestry. Open my eyes to see the way you designed me. Help me to pay attention to what I do well and what I find satisfying. Thank you for allowing me to feel joy when I do what you've designed me to do, so that I'll seek to do that thing again and again. As I do it, may I serve you and may I accomplish the good works that you intended for me from all eternity. I praise you for your gifts in the name of the Lord Jesus Christ.

Session Three
STUDY YOUR S.T.O.R.Y.

Getting Started

Giftedness is what we do naturally because God designed us to function that way. We're using our giftedness when we're in our sweet spots. In the activity below, we're continuing the process of storytelling that we've been following for the previous two sessions in an effort to uncover our sweet spots. As before, turn to the person next to you and tell him or her about one of the activities from your sweet spot activity list. Again, it's best if you can share with someone whom you haven't talked with yet. If you have not made a list, go back to a time in your past and recall an activity that you enjoyed doing and feel you did well. Follow the instructions below to tell the other person how you went about that activity and what you found so satisfying about it.

What Do We Mean by "Naturally"?

Giftedness is what we do naturally. But some wonder, is that a good thing? In 1 Corinthians, Paul uses the term "natural" to describe someone who is not in Christ, and "spiritual" to describe someone who is in Christ. For that reason, it is not uncommon for some Christians to frown upon the term "natural." They equate "natural" with "sinful."

But "natural" doesn't mean "sinful." Instead, it refers to the condition we were in when we were born. When Paul was describing a "natural" person, he meant someone who was still in the same condition in which he was born— that is, in his natural state, which means apart from Christ. So it *is* consistent with Paul to say that giftedness is "natural." That means it is inborn. We come into the world with our giftedness because God fashioned us in the womb and designed us uniquely (Ps. 139).

Sharing and Listening Activity 1

1. Tell the person next to you about a time in your past when you did an activity that you enjoyed doing and feel you did well. Describe *what* you did and *how* you went about doing it. Do not go *into* why you did it. Just narrate what the other person would have seen you doing, as if a camcorder had been there to capture the action.

2. As you've done in the previous sessions, describe the satisfaction you gained from the activity. Be specific. What was it about that activity that felt so satisfying?

When Person 1 is finished, turn the conversation around. Person 2 should now respond to (1) and (2) above.

Looking for Your S.T.O.R.Y.

In *Cure for the Common Life*, Max provides a framework for examining your stories to see a recurring pattern. There are five things to look for in your stories, represented by the letters S.T.O.R.Y., as follows:

S: What are your **Strengths**? What are the action words (or verbs) that you use to describe what you did. For example: "I planned," "I spoke," "I taught," "I built." We see your **Strengths** when you are in action.

T: What is your **Topic**? What are the things you work on, with, or through in your stories? For example: numbers, plants, machinery, money, a team, an audience, a concept, a language. We see your **Topic** in the things to which you apply **Strengths**.

O: What are your **Optimal Conditions**? What's the environment in which you thrive? For example: structure, crises, instructions, projects, potential, goals. We see your **Optimal Conditions** in the circumstances of your sweet spot.

R: What is your preferred **Relationship**? What relationship to others do you usually take on in your stories? Are you the person in charge, a follower, a collaborator, a team contributor, a Lone Ranger? We see your preferred **Relationship** in the role you like to play in your stories.

Y: What is your **Yes!**? What is the satisfaction you felt in your stories? What ultimate outcome gave you the most enjoyment? We see your **Yes!** in what made your activity seem worth doing.

FAQ

Q: What is S.T.O.R.Y. really about?

A: There's a lot of talk nowadays about the concept of "passion." But what does that term really mean? *Passion* is a feeling, a subjective response to an activity one finds pleasurable and would probably do again. It's great to feel passionate about something, but not everyone feels that way. In fact, some people don't feel particularly passionate about anything. Yet everyone has a *giftedness*, which has more to do with the unique way in which they function and behave than how they feel. A person will take satisfaction from an activity that makes good use of their giftedness. They may even become "passionate" about that activity. But the thing to pay attention to is the underlying motivation and core strengths they use to do that activity, more than their feelings about the activity. S.T.O.R.Y. helps identify the giftedness that accounts for whatever satisfaction or passion a person feels.

Reflecting

- Take a moment to write in the space provided what you found so satisfying in the activity you shared about with your partner.

• Take a moment to write down in the space provided some of the action words (or verbs) you used to accomplish your activity.

Sharing and Listening Activity 2

Let's tell another story. If there's a period of your life from which you have not yet told a story, try to pick a story from that period. For example, if most of your stories have been from your youth, try to pick a story from more recent years. If most of your stories have been from adulthood, try to pick a story from your youth. Remember, the key is that you found the activity satisfying.

1. As before, tell the person next to you about a time in your past when you did an activity that you enjoyed doing and feel you did well. Describe *what* you did and *how* you went about doing it.

2. Describe the satisfaction you gained from the activity. Be specific. What was it about the activity that felt so satisfying?

When Person 1 is finished, turn the conversation around. Person 2 should now respond to (1) and (2) above.

Focusing

- Take a moment to write down in the space provided what you found so satisfying in the activity you just told about.

- Take a moment to write down in the space provided some of the action words (or verbs) you used to accomplish your activity.

Sharing and Listening Activity 3

Let's tell one more story in this session, using the same process. Tell the person next to you about one of the activities from your list of sweet spot activities. Or, if you don't have a list, go back to a time in your past and recall an activity that you enjoyed doing and feel you did well.

1. As before, tell the person next to you about a time in your past when you did an activity that you enjoyed doing and feel you did well. Describe what you did and how you went about doing it.

2. Describe the satisfaction you gained from the activity. Be specific. What was it about the activity that felt so satisfying?

When Person 1 is finished, turn the conversation around. Person 2 should now respond to (1) and (2) above.

Discovering

- Take a moment to write down in the space provided what you found so satisfying in the activity you just told about.

• Take a moment to write down in the space provided in your guide some of the action words (or verbs) you used to accomplish your activity.

• You now have a number of sweet spot stories to look at. Does anyone notice any similarities between the stories you've told during these first three sessions? Describe those similarities.

Hint: Use the S.T.O.R.Y. framework to look for things that repeat and recur among the stories. For instance, perhaps the same Topics keep showing up—like animals, or machinery, or numbers. Or maybe the same Strengths keep showing up—for example, performing, crafting, or reading. If you see a pattern emerging, make note of it so you can share with your partner.

- By listening to the person next to you tell his stories, you've now seen three snapshots of that person in his sweet spot. Take a moment to tell the person next to you what you see him doing when in his sweet spot.

Pulling It Together

By now, you're probably starting to get pretty familiar with what you look like when you're in your sweet spot. For some people, the sweet spot is very apparent. For others, it is much more subtle. So how do you nail down a description of your sweet spot? By telling stories and looking for patterns. You've told half a dozen stories or more by now. And you can always tell more. You've also examined those stories a little bit with the help of others in the group. Between now and the next session, use the activity on the following page to help you look closer at your stories and see what patterns you can detect.

> Consider yourself a million-dollar investment—in many cases, a multi-million-dollar enterprise.
>
> God gives gifts, not miserly, but abundantly.
>
> And not randomly, but carefully: "to each according to his ability" (Matt. 25:15 NIV).
>
> Remember, no one else has your talents. No one. God elevates you from commonhood by matching your unique abilities to custom-made assignments.
>
> – Max Lucado

Finding a Sweet Spot Partner

You can learn a great deal more from your stories if you examine them with a partner. Who should be that partner? Here are some qualities to look for in a partner:

- **Objectivity.** Choose someone who can stick with what you are saying, not what she is feeling or thinking. This process needs to be about you, not her. Family members will not make the best sweet spot partners because they'll tend to view the story from their perspectives. They may also cause you to tell the story in a biased way, according to underlying family patterns of interaction.

- **Insight.** Select someone who is able to see patterns and themes that repeat in your stories.

- **Maturity.** Seek out someone who appreciates that you are trying to learn about yourself. He needs to take you seriously and take the process seriously.

- **Honesty.** Pick someone who doesn't mind telling you what she sees in your stories. This process is intended to get at truth about you—the positive truth about you—so it makes sense to recruit a partner who is able to tell the truth.

- **Understanding.** Choose someone who will take a genuine interest in you. Even though you are telling about the best moments of your life, there is still a degree of vulnerability involved in this process. You need someone who will not be critical or judgmental, but instead empathetic.

- **Ability to follow the process.** Recruit someone who will stick to the storytelling guidelines spelled out in this small group study. The process is simple, but works well when it is followed. If it is not followed, it doesn't work.

For the Next Session

1. Review the sweet spot activities you talked about in the first three sessions of the group. If you'd like, find an objective partner to help you examine your stories and look for patterns in them.

   - What similarities do you see among your stories?

   - What activities do you keep coming back to again and again?

- Are there any action words (verbs) that keep repeating in your stories?

- Is there a particular role that you enjoy playing in your stories (for example: advisor, helper, cheerleader, idea originator, problem solver, etc.)?

- Are there any common themes about the satisfaction you take from your sweet spot activities?

Lord, certain activities seem to fit me quite naturally, and for that reason I don't pay much attention to those activities, or what they reveal about me. In fact, even now, after telling several stories and looking for patterns of giftedness, I may not think that what I'm seeing is very significant. Yet your Word tells me that what I do best is the result of your design, and that you've designed me the way you have because you have specific good works you've appointed me to do. Lord, help me to pay attention to my giftedness, and to celebrate it for what it is—a gift from your hand, with which to love and serve you.

Session Four
TAKE YOUR JOB AND LOVE IT

Getting Started

Our giftedness has huge implications on where and how we invest our lives—paid employment or not. Ephesians 2:10 says that God prepared "good works" for us to do in this world, and one of the main places we do those good works—or should be doing them—is in our work. As in all areas of our lives, we should seek to do most what we do best in our work lives as well.

For the next activity, work in groups of three. Following the directions below, tell the people in your group about one of the activities from your sweet spot activity list that you have not yet talked about. Or, if you prefer, choose a story that you didn't put on the list, but you know describes an activity that you enjoyed doing and feel you did well. Tell the others how you went about that activity, and what you found so satisfying about it.

No Talent? No Way!

God has made each one of us just the way we are, with just the right combination of abilities and motivation to do our own unique thing. And if you get into a job that doesn't ask for your combination of abilities and motivation, then you probably won't do so well. You certainly won't feel energized by the work, and you probably won't enjoy it very much, either.

Does that mean there's something wrong with you? No! It means your work is asking you for strengths you don't have, qualities that God didn't give you. That doesn't make you an untalented person—it means you may be "mis-positioned." It means you may be out of your sweet spot.

If that's the case, take heart! Instead of beating yourself up, look around and see if you can find a job that fits you better. Because the truth about you is this: there is something *right* with you. It's called your giftedness. And God wants you to use your giftedness to make a contribution somewhere in this world.

Sharing and Listening Activity 1

1. **Person 1:** Tell the people in your group about an activity you did in your life that you enjoyed doing and feel you did well. Describe *what* you did and *how* you went about doing it. Do not go into *why* you did it. Just narrate what the other person would have seen you doing.

2. Describe the satisfaction you gained from the activity. Be specific. What was it about that activity that felt so satisfying?

3. When the story is complete, Persons 2 and 3 should each tell the storyteller what they heard the main satisfaction was from the activity discussed. Person 1 should write down what they say in the journal space below.

4. Next, Persons 2 and 3 should tell the storyteller what action words (or verbs) they heard her use to describe what she did. Person 1 should write down what they say in the journal space below.

Now, rotate. Repeat the storytelling activity outlined in steps 1–4 above for the other two people in the group.

Working Matters

Max writes,

God's eyes fall on the work of our hands. Our Wednesdays matter to him as much as our Sundays. He blurs the secular and sacred. One stay-at-home mom keeps this sign over her kitchen sink: *Divine tasks performed here, daily.* An executive hung this plaque in her office: *My desk is my altar.* Both are correct. With God, our work matters as much as our worship. Indeed, work can be worship. (*Cure for the Common Life*, pages 97-98)

If that's true (and it is), then doesn't it make sense that we should try to find as good a fit as possible between our work and the giftedness that God has given us?

Take a moment to look back over your sweet spot stories, both the ones you've told to others in the group, as well as the rest of those on your sweet spot activity list. How many of those stories come from your work life—whether in paid employment or in working in the home? If few of your stories are work-related, pay attention to that. It could mean that you're not finding as much satisfaction in your day-to-day work as you could. If that's the case, it suggests a mis-fit between who you are and what you are being asked to do all day.

What Do We Mean by "Good Fit"?

Ever worn an item of clothing that didn't fit quite right? Perhaps it was a sweater that was way too big and made you feel like the Abominable Snowman. Or maybe it was a pair of shorts that were much too tight and left you doing your best imitation of a stuffed sausage. In either case, you probably felt very uncomfortable.

In the same way, sometimes a job just doesn't fit right. A job doesn't "fit" when it's either too *loose*—in that it makes no use of the God-given strengths and motivation we bring to it, or if it's too *tight*—in that it feels constricting and demands strengths and motivations that God didn't give us.

None of us gets the perfect job-fit this side of heaven. Still, some jobs fit us better than others, and it makes sense to pursue a better fit than a not-so-good fit. If we work at a job that fits us well, we'll put our all into it and seek to do our best. We'll also gain satisfaction from it.

Colossians 3:23 (NAS) exhorts us to "do your work heartily," that is, to put your heart into your job, because you're ultimately serving the Lord in your position. We need to put our hearts into our jobs no matter what those jobs are. But let's face it—it will be a lot easier to put our hearts into our work if our hearts are naturally drawn to our work. That's what it means to have a good job-fit—*the work fits both our motivation and our abilities.*

A lot of people ask, "What's the 'right' job for me?" Granted, very few people get to have their "perfect" job. But clearly some jobs are more "right" for us than others. How can we tell what those better job-fits are? The answer is to look at our giftedness. Think back over your sweet spot stories. What are the common threads among your stories? Those threads will point to what you do best. A "better job-fit" is one that makes good use of what you do best.

Let's go back into our groups and talk about what a "better job-fit" looks like for each of us.

Sweet Spots and the Stay-at-Home Parent

If you're a stay-at-home parent, you may feel like this session on finding your sweet spot at work doesn't apply to you. But it does. Your sweet spot is every bit as useful in parenting as it would be if you were in paid employment.

As you fill your role as a mother or father, the parts of the job that fit your sweet spot will feel satisfying and productive. Likewise, the parts that don't fit so well will take more energy and feel less rewarding. But that would be the case in any other job, as well.

"But I was born to be a mother," a woman might say. "That's my gifted-ness." Well, not necessarily. It's great to enjoy being a mother, but recognize that motherhood is a *role*, not an *identity*. Your identity has to do with your God-given personhood. That's where your giftedness resides—in your essential personhood. The mothering role may fit you well because it makes good use of gifts you naturally possess. If so, rejoice in that.

What if you're not a "born parent"? Not all people are. If you're not, don't shame yourself. Be the best mom or dad you can be by fulfilling the role God has assigned you as best you can, even if a lot of it is made of "can dos" rather than "love to dos." Your giftedness may find a better expression outside the home, and that's fine. God knew what he was doing when he put you together.

We'd probably all like to be "the perfect parent." But in parenting, as in every other activity, some people just naturally do it better than others. Why? You guessed it: Because of their giftedness.

Sharing and Listening Activity 2

1. Based on my sweet spot stories, how would I describe what I do best? Consider using elements from the S.T.O.R.Y. outline to give a more complete description:

   S: What are your *Strengths*? (Action words or verbs)

   T: What is your *Topic*? (Things you work on, with, or through)

   O: What are your *Optimal* conditions? (Environment in which you thrive)

   R: What is your preferred *Relationship*? (Role that fits you best)

   Y: What is your *Yes!*? (Most satisfying ultimate outcome)

"I'd work best in a job where I could

use my abilities for figuring things out and influencing,	SKILLS
to work on machinery and equipment,	TOPIC
under tight deadlines and pressure,	OPTIMAL CONDITIONS
and on my own,	RELATIONSHIPS
in order to see improvement and feel like I'd saved the day."	YES!

2. How could you phrase your description in terms of a job? For example: "I'd work best in a job where I could use my abilities for figuring things out and influencing to work on machinery and equipment, under tight deadlines and pressure, and on my own, in order to see improvement and feel like I'd saved the day."

Hint: Avoid using occupational titles in this exercise (e.g. lawyer, accountant, mechanic, salesperson). Your sweet spot is not limited to a single occupation. It can be used in numerous occupations. Occupational titles are limiting and vague. Someone could say, "I should be a doctor." But what sort of doctor? There is considerable difference between the work of an emergency room specialist, a pathologist, a pediatrician, and a psychiatrist. And even within those specializations physicians work in many different settings. One pediatrician practices in a small town in the country, another in a suburban community, and another in a clinic in the inner city. Try to describe your ideal job in terms of the giftedness first. Then you can look in the real world to consider occupations that might fit you.

What Do I Do Best?

Examples:

- I love to work outdoors with my hands and my body, building things and putting things together, with a team of guys who are working to complete the job and get it right.

- The best way to use me is to put me with a group of people and get them brainstorming. I love to help people come up with new ideas, and then put a plan together to make those ideas happen. That's the biggest thrill for me—to see a plan come together and do something really exciting.

- What I do best is to talk people into buying things. I'm particularly good at tangible things, like cars, real estate, jewelry, etc. I need to have some competition, and I need to work independently. What I find most satisfying is to get that positive response, that "yes" from the customer. That's when I know I've done my job.

- I would be best with groups of children, teaching them to read and write, and also to get along with one another. I do that best in a classroom setting with a curriculum to follow, but with some creativity and adaptation allowed on my part. I'm glad to be with the children alone, as long as I have a supportive team to go back to. I get satisfaction out of seeing the kids light up with excitement when they can see their progress.

- I'm basically a team player. Give me a group of people and a job to do and I'm happy. There are a lot of needs in this world, and they won't get met unless folks partner up and get after them. That's what I want to do. Let's not just talk about helping people, let's do it!

- My best use is to analyze financial data and economic factors in order to predict what's going to happen in financial markets. I guess the ideal conditions for me are a fast-paced environment with lots of uncertainty, with everyone relying on me. I need total focus and concentration. What I love is the challenge, the way I am personally tested every day to see if I can make an accurate forecast.

- I'm best at organization. I want to be in an office where things need to be organized, structured, planned, and scheduled. I want to feel like I'm a vital part of a team. I serve the team by keeping them on track. That's very satisfying, to know that we're reaching our goals because I kept things organized.

- I've always loved books, ever since I was a little kid. So now I know my best use is to read and study, and then tell people what I've learned. I usually do that through writing, but I can also explain what I know in a presentation. I need someone else to get the people together and set up the program. But once that's done, I'm ready to go. I love helping people understand new ideas and new ways of looking at things.

3. Imagine that you actually were working in the "what I do best" job that you just described. How would that help you "do your work heartily, as to the Lord" (Col. 3:23 NKJV)?

4. How does the description you just gave compare with the job you currently have (or, if unemployed, your last job and other jobs you have held)?

5. Based on what the others in your group have heard from your stories, how do they respond to your descriptions for questions 1 and 2? Would they add or change anything?

As Good a Fit as Possible

All of us can imagine our dream job. Playing on the PGA circuit against Tiger Woods. Managing the hammock shop in Maui. Serving as the Chief Taste Tester for Godiva Chocolates. We can easily dream about the perfect job for us, the one that fits our giftedness to a tee. But is that the job we should hold out for?

Actually, no. Not that there's anything wrong with conceiving of the ideal job for our sweet spot. But in this world we have to make peace with the fact that the best fit conceivable is not necessarily the best fit achievable. The world will not always accommodate our desire to find the ideal job. In fact, it will not accommodate us most of the time.

This is an important reality to accept. We live in a fallen world, which by definition means that we don't get everything we'd like this side of heaven. That's okay. Even in a fallen world, God has a purpose for us—a purpose for which he has designed us. The most prudent path we can follow is this: First, identify our giftedness as best we can. Then we need to look intensively and intentionally in the world to find opportunities that fit that giftedness, given the personal realities on our plate. Then we need to pursue the best available option.

So, if our personal reality dictates that we have a family to provide for, then we need to seek a job that provides for them. In picking that job, we should consider what jobs are available that will do that. Among those jobs, we should consider the one that best matches our giftedness. Why? Because we will do better work in that job. That's what God wants us to do: good work, using our giftedness on the opportunities he brings our way. The key is that we use our giftedness as best we can where we *are*, not the best we can imagine using it where we *are not*.

Creating a Better Fit

It's fun to imagine working in the ideal job. But we live in the real world, and few people get to have their "perfect" job. So how do we make the best of a job that may be far from a perfect fit? How can we make the best of the job we have? Here are four strategies to consider:

- **Add.** Try to add a task or responsibility to your job that you know you will do well and find satisfying. You will gain energy from that to do the less satisfying parts.

- **Subtract.** Try to subtract some of the less satisfying parts of your job and get them off your plate. Are there things you are doing that someone else would be much better suited to do?

- **Multiply.** Multiply the energy you have available for bringing to work by doing something in your sweet spot outside of your work.

- **Divide.** Take a task for which you are not well suited and try to divide that load by finding someone who has the giftedness you lack and enlisting him to help you.

What If I'm Out of Work?

"I don't care about having the perfect job. I'll take any job. I need work!" That's probably what you're thinking as you hear about making the best of your job. Never mind the "perfect" part—you'd be happy just to have a job to make the best of.

If you're out of work, keep in mind four truths:

(1) **You still have a sweet spot.** Unemployment doesn't change who you are. To be sure, your self-esteem can take a blow when you can't find work. But God made you, with all of your gifts and talents, long before you became unemployed. He made you as you are for a purpose. Don't let temporary setbacks allow you to doubt that.

(2) **The reason you are out of work may have nothing to do with your giftedness.** The unemployed person is tempted to think, "There's something wrong with me. That's why I'm out of work. I'm not smart enough, strong enough, energetic enough, creative enough, or whatever." Stop! The voice telling you that is not the Lord's. So don't keep listening to that voice. Instead, accept the fact that we live in an imperfect world, and there is no such thing as guaranteed employment. Economies run in cycles. Businesses fail. Companies change. Markets require different ways of doing business. None of that is a

reflection of who you are. Adjust to the ebb and flow of employment as best you can, but don't disparage your giftedness.

(3) **It is a biblical admonition to provide for your family.** One reason God gives us work is so that we can meet our material needs (2 Thess. 3:6–12). That means we need to do what we can to find work that meets our needs. If your situation is desperate, you shouldn't hold out for the absolutely perfect job. Take a job and do it faithfully, all the while keeping your eyes open for a better job-fit when it comes along. And above all. . .

(4) **Trust God.** That can be hard to do when there are bills to pay and no income with which to pay them. But consider this: God is less interested in our material comfort than in our spiritual vitality. It may be that he allows us to be out of work sometimes in order to get our attention, and to get our eyes refocused on him. Are you looking for him in the midst of your job search?

Sharing and Listening Activity 3

Work through the following questions for each person in the group:

1. How did you describe your "what I do best" job in the previous activity?

2. Based on that description, describe some of the things that don't fit well in your current job (or, if unemployed, your last job and other jobs you have held).

Hint: As you describe what doesn't fit in your job, beware of two extremes. On the one hand, avoid being overly negative and critical about your job, your supervisor, or your employer. Just stick to what your sweet spot is all about, and talk about ways in which your sweet spot doesn't match the expectations or the conditions at work.

On the other hand, avoid shying away from legitimate areas of mis-fit between you and your job out of fear that you might be saying something unkind or unfair. As with the person who is overly negative, so with you: be honest about your sweet spot, and talk about ways in which your sweet spot doesn't match the expectations or the conditions at work.

3. Given the four strategies mentioned—Add, Subtract, Multiply, and Divide—which of those strategies do you think would be best for you to use in making the best of your less-than-ideal job-fit? Give an example below of how you might make that strategy work.

> In a desire to be great, one might cease being any good. Not every teacher is equipped to be a principal. Not every carpenter has the skill to head a crew. Not every musician should conduct an orchestra. Promotions might promote a person right out of his or her sweet spot. For the love of more, we might lose our purpose.
>
> – Max Lucado

Pulling It Together

The tendency in our society is to think that the "best" job is the one that pays the most. But that's not how God sees it. He certainly wants us to earn a living and provide for our needs. But he has gifted each of us differently because there are so many things that need to be done in this world.

We need teachers, nurses, mechanics, airline pilots, financial investors, truck drivers, crane operators, toll-booth collectors, police, and fire fighters. All honest labor matters to God. He has fit each of us for certain kinds of work. And so to the degree we have options, we should seek out and do the work for which God has fitted us. That is one of the primary ways we can serve and bring glory to God.

For the Next Session

1. Review your description of your "what I do best" job on page 54. Go back to your stories and what you learned about yourself from them and see if you can refine that description into a clear statement of the job you would do best.

2. Show your refined description of your "what I do best" job to someone who knows you well. Discuss the implications of that description for your current job, as well as for your future jobs.

3. Talk with that same person about the strategy you could use to make the best of your less-than-ideal job-fit. How can you get started on implementing that strategy right away?

Lord, thank you that all my work matters to you. Thank you for fitting me to do certain kinds of work. Help me to seek out and find the best job-fit I can, so that in my work, as in all of my life, I will do most what I do best. Lord, if I need a job, help me to find one. And if I have a job, but find it hard to believe that job could be part of the "good works" you intended for me to do, then help me to look at my job the way you see it.

Session Five

DISCOVER YOUR ROLE

Getting Started

God made us to live in community. That's why we have families and groups of friends, neighborhoods and towns, cities and suburbs, tribes and nations. It's vital to our God-given nature to be connected with other people. But here we come to an interesting reality: the way in which each of us relates to others is as unique as everything else about us. Some of us just assume that we should be in charge, while others assume that someone else should be in charge. Some of us like to do things by ourselves, others wouldn't think of doing anything apart from a group. Some of us require a specific role to play, others are happy to play almost any role that's needed.

Each of us relate to others in our own, unique way, and there's no one "right" way to relate to others—except, of course, to treat one another with love. But how we do that differs according to our giftedness. Those to whom God has given leadership gifts love others by leading. Those who've been given administrative gifts love others through organization. Those who've been given the gifts of serving love others by meeting their needs. Everyone has been given a way to relate to others. We need everyone's contribution, and we need to honor everyone's contribution. That's what we're going to focus on in this session. We want to consider how our sweet spot affects the way we relate to other people in our lives.

This time, for a different perspective, let's partner up by gender: men with men, and women with women. Follow the activity below to tell your partner about one of your sweet spot activities—how you went about the activity, and what you found so satisfying about it.

Sharing and Listening Activity 1

1. **Person 1:** Tell your partner about an activity you've done that you enjoyed doing and feel you did well. Describe *what* you did and *how* you went about doing it. Do not go into *why* you did it. Just narrate what the other person would have seen you doing.

2. Describe the satisfaction you gained from the activity. Be specific. What was it about that activity that felt so satisfying?

3. When the story is complete, allow your partner to tell you what he heard as the main satisfaction that you gained from the activity. In determining that satisfaction, the listener should consider the entire story in addition to what you said in response to the question in step 2 above.

    As your partner answers that question, write down a summary of what he says in the space provided.

4. Next, your partner should tell you what action words (or verbs) he heard you use to describe what you did.

As before, write down what the listener says in the space provided.

When Person 1 is finished, turn the conversation around. Person 2 should now work through steps 1–4 above.

FAQ

Q: How do genetics factor into my giftedness?

A: The short answer is: we don't yet know. The phenomenon of giftedness has been around for as long as there have been human beings, but only within the past half-century has anyone started to investigate it. It's still too early to know how DNA and giftedness are related, if at all.

However, giftedness allows us to think about ourselves as more than just the product of our parents' DNA. Giftedness shows that God has designed us with a *purpose* in mind. He has fitted us for particular tasks that he wants accomplished in this world. In effect, each of us is a brand new idea from heaven!

Expanding Our View

By now we've told a number of sweet spot stories. Hopefully we've started to see some patterns in the way we behave when we're in our sweet spot. In telling our stories thus far, we've focused primarily on ourselves as individuals—what *we* did in our stories. Now we'll consider the other people involved in those stories. Who were the people around us when we were in our sweet spot? There's a lot to be gained by noticing those other people, and paying attention to how we behaved *in relation to them*. In this session, we'll begin to see how our sweet spot significantly affects the way we interact with others.

Sharing and Listening Activity 2

1. Look back over all of the sweet spot stories you have told during the five sessions of this discussion group. Identify any other people who were a part of your stories. If there aren't other people in one or more of your stories, make note of that.

2. With your partner, try to identify a pattern to how other people fit into your stories. Here are some questions to consider:

    (a) Did you work on, with, or through people to accomplish your sweet spot?

    Examples:
    - I seem to work with children in a lot of my stories.
    - I'm always working with small groups and teams in my stories.
    - I'm up in front of audiences quite a bit in my stories.

(b) What strengths or abilities did you use in working with people?

Examples:

- I seem to do a lot of teaching when I'm with people in my stories.

- My stories show that I like to try and figure people out—to get inside their heads and understand them in order to help them.

- I'm a born salesperson. My stories show me always trying to get people to buy something—a cup of lemonade, a ticket to a school dance, a new idea, etc.

(c) What role do you characteristically play relative to other people in your stories?

Examples:

- I seem to be a sparkplug in a lot of my stories, the person who gets everyone excited and energized.

- I'm basically a team player in almost all my stories. I don't have to lead the team, I just have to be on a team.

- I seem to be fairly independent in my stories. I do my own thing and don't really work with others to get things done.

HINT: Be careful not to make judgments about yourself from what your stories reveal about the way you relate to other people. You may see some things you've never recognized about yourself. Perhaps you never realized how much you like to be in charge, or how much you need a collaborator, or how important it is for you to work independently. Accept whatever the stories show. Don't dismiss legitimate insights with the attitude, "Well, I know I was that way in the stories, but I *should* relate to people in some other, more 'acceptable' way." No! There is no "should" for you except for the way God made you. You *should* be that person. That includes the way he made you to relate to others. Be who you are!

3. See if you can summarize the role you prefer to play when you're in your sweet spot into a simple phrase or slogan. Some examples: "crisis manager," "scheduler," "the man with the facts," "deadline-meeter," "key advisor," "values champion," "wordsmith." (Caution: Do not use negative labels, even in humor.)

When Person 1 is finished, turn the conversation around. Person 2 should now work through steps 1–3 above with your partner.

Moses had a staff.
David had a sling.
Samson had a jawbone.
Rahab had a string.
Mary had some ointment.
Aaron had a rod.
Dorcas had a needle.
All were used by God.
What do you have?

– Max Lucado

Sharing and Listening Activity 3

1. **Person 1:** Look back at your responses to the previous activity. Can you give an example or two of how your preferred way of relating to others shows up in one of your current relationships? (For example: at home with your spouse or a child, at work with a supervisor or coworker, in a volunteer position at church.)

2. How does your preferred way of relating to others enable you to live in your sweet spot?

3. In what ways do you think your preferred way of relating to others might negatively affect your relationships or create problems for others? Can you or your partner think of ways you might avoid that, without trying to change who you are?

When Person 1 is finished, turn the conversation around. Person 2 should now work through steps 1–3 above with your partner.

Reflecting

As we think about the ways in which we relate to other people while we are in our sweet spots, it's important to remember that there are no "right" or "wrong" answers when it comes to our preferred roles. Our tendency as human beings is to think that everyone should relate to others the way we relate to others. But God has not designed us to do that. He's made each of us to be unique. And so we relate to others in very different ways.

Some of us were made to be the life of the party. Some of us were made to be in charge. Some of us were made to work in the background. Some of us were made to wait until a key moment comes along, and then we jump in with an important contribution. Some of us were made to be team players. Some of us were made to be Lone Rangers.

This is a valuable truth for us to grasp. Each of us is unique. Each of us has a unique contribution to make. That means that every one of us is needed. As 1 Corinthians 12:21–22 NIV says, "The eye cannot say to the hand, 'I don't need you!' And the head cannot say to the feet, 'I don't need you!' On the contrary, those parts of the body that seem to be weaker are indispensable." That's a strong word: *indispensable*. That means there's no one we can do without. Every one of us has value.

Think over the stories you analyzed to develop your S.T.O.R.Y. What "small things" did God use to lead you into some experience of success or joy? How did he use these small things? The truth is, we often find patterns not only in the ways our lives unfold but also in the way God frequently chooses to deal with us, often through other people. What patterns do you find, if any, in the way God has used small things to impact you and those around you? Begin looking for how God might want to use other small things in your life for his glory and your benefit. Pray that he will open your eyes and motivate you to action.

Sharing and Listening Activity 4

1. **Person 1:** Given what you do best (your sweet spot), who is "indispensable" for you? Who do you need around you to complement your strengths? One way to figure that out is to ask: *What are the things that I am not naturally motivated to do?* or *What things do I not do well?* The things you are not naturally motivated to do and do not do well are things that other people *are* designed to do, and they can complement your strengths.

2. Sometimes the people who complement your strengths may actually frustrate you a bit, because they are so different from you. How does seeing those people in light of their giftedness affect your opinion of them? What ways can you and your partner think of to affirm those people in their giftedness?

When Person 1 is finished, turn the conversation around. Person 2 should now work through steps 1–2 above.

Pulling It Together

In these sessions we've seen how each of us has a sweet spot because of the way God has made us. In fact, every human being has a unique sweet spot. Consider what that means: Every time you interact with other people, your sweet spot is interacting with their sweet spots.

Think about the relationships you have in your life—with your spouse, your kids, your parents and siblings, your grandparents, your friends, your coworkers, your neighbors, your church family, your pastor. Every single one of those people has a unique sweet spot. And every time you relate to them, your sweet spot and their sweet spots interact. Sometimes those interactions are quite productive; sometimes they are not productive at all. But it's important to see that at the heart of each one of us is something special—a desire, a drive that God has put in us to motivate us to do the thing for which he created us. We need to discover those special gifts in one another, and we need to celebrate them when we do. Most importantly, we need to invite one another to use our gifts.

For the Next Session

1. Talk with someone who knows you well—your spouse, a friend, a family member—about what your stories reveal about the way you prefer to relate to others.

2. Reflect on the key relationships you currently have in your life. How does your sweet spot affect those relationships—for better or for worse? How can you build those relationships without changing who you are?

Lord, thank you for all of the people you have brought into my life—my family, my friends, my coworkers, my fellow church members, my neighbors. Thank you for the way you have made each one of them. Help me to pay attention to each person's uniqueness, even as I pay attention to my own uniqueness. Help me to be who you intended me to be, and help me invite others to be who you intended them to be. I need your help, because I do not have everything it takes to understand other people fully or relate to them perfectly. Help me to honor those who have strengths I don't have. And help me to use the strengths you have given me to bring grace to other people.

Session Six
BE THE BODY

Getting Started

We've come to the final session in our small group study. We've covered a lot of ground! We've told stories. We've learned about living in our sweet spots. In this session we'll apply what we know about our sweet spots to the activities we accomplish through our churches.

God has placed local churches in the world to be centers of light and life to their surrounding communities. It is through churches that God brings the gospel to people around the world. That means that churches have a lot of jobs that need to be done—most of them on a voluntary basis. Some of those jobs involve "inside" work and some involve "outside" work. The "inside" jobs include all of the tasks required to maintain a thriving community of faith among the people who are already a part of the church: jobs like teaching Sunday school classes, singing in the choir, ushering, parking cars, ordering books for the church library, raising money for new facilities, and so on. The "outside" jobs include the tasks required to reach out to the community and the world with the love of Christ: jobs like organizing and staging an evangelistic rally, mentoring a young person at a youth center, volunteering at a crisis pregnancy center, assisting at a homeless shelter, helping to build a house for a needy family, or planning a missions trip.

In this session, we want to consider where our sweet spot can make its best contribution in our churches. Some of us will take on "inside" roles, others will take on "outside" roles, and some of us may do both. But all of us are needed. Indeed, God gave us our gifts to serve him in and through the church.

Sharing and Listening Activity 1

1. **Person 1:** Tell your partner about an activity you did in your life that you enjoyed doing and feel you did well. Describe *what* you did and *how* you went about doing it. Do not go into *why* you did it. Just narrate what the other person would have seen you doing.

2. Describe the satisfaction you gained from the activity. Be specific. What was it about that activity that felt so satisfying?

3. When the story is complete, allow your partner to tell you what she heard as the main satisfaction that you gained from the activity. As your partner answers that question, write down a summary of what she says in the space provided.

4. Next, your partner should tell you what action words (or verbs) she heard you use to describe what you did. As before, write down what the listener says in the space provided.

When Person 1 is finished, turn the conversation around. Person 2 should now work through steps 1–4 above with your partner.

Focusing

In the last session, you paid particular attention to the way you relate to others when you're in your sweet spot. You saw that you usually prefer to play a particular role in relation to other people. As you think about the work of your church, it's important that you play the role God has specially designed for you. That's what Paul tells us to do in Romans 12, where he likens the church to a human body: "For as we have many members in one body but all the members do not have the same function, so we, being many, are one body in Christ, and individually members one of

> A 3 AM diaper change fits in very few sweet spots. Most S.T.O.R.Y.'s don't feature the strength of garage sweeping. Visiting your sick neighbor might not come naturally to you. Still, the sick need to be encouraged, garages need sweeping, and diapers need changing.
>
> – Max Lucado

another. Having then gifts according to the grace that is given to us, let us use them" (verses 4–6 NKJV).

Sharing and Listening Activity 2

1. Look back to Session Five, Sharing and Listening Activity 2, question 3 on page 75. What role do you typically prefer to play when you're in your sweet spot?

2. With your partner, brainstorm some ways that you might play that role in the life and work of your local church. Some examples are listed below.

   Examples:

   - I like to be a team contributor. I could do that as a member of the parking team.

   - I'm a person who likes to initiate action and get things going. I could do that by heading up a task force on one of the church's committees.

   - I'm basically a salesperson who likes to get a response. I could do that as a greeter on Sunday mornings, greeting people as they arrive at church.

   - I'm always the planner in my sweet spots. Our church has scheduled a "work day" at a community center in the inner city, and I could help plan that day.

- I like to be the one who explains things, especially in writing. I could help publicize our church's work to the community by writing up stories about what we're doing and sending them to our local newspaper.

Hint: As you and your partner brainstorm together, think about what your church is trying to accomplish. Perhaps it has a mission statement, or a particular emphasis, or has recently launched a certain initiative. How might your sweet spot contribute to that end?

When Person 1 is finished, turn the conversation around. Person 2 should now work through steps 1–2 above with your partner.

God grants us an uncommon life to the degree we surrender our common one.

– Max Lucado

Considering Your Strengths

Look at the following various scenarios. Which situation(s) best fits your strengths?

(1) We need someone to get an office organized—papers filed, equipment set up properly, contents of drawers put in order, things labeled accurately, and so on.

(2) An emergency strikes. We need someone with a clear head to assess the situation, formulate a plan for response, mobilize people, and get things under control.

(3) A neighbor is going through a divorce. She is past the shock of it, but feels like she needs someone to talk to. We need someone who can listen and respond calmly and wisely to what she has to say.

(4) A youth group from the church is going on a mission trip to help rebuild a church that was damaged in a hurricane. We need someone to go as an assistant to the youth leaders and help keep the kids on task.

(5) We need someone to figure out what has broken down on an old bus and, if possible, get it running again.

(6) A group of men in the church have organized a softball team and joined a league. They need someone to coach the team.

(7) The women's ministry is getting ready to hold a conference. We need someone to put together a notebook for the conference attendees that will hold all of their notes, presentation slides, and additional information for the conference.

(8) A longtime leader of a civic organization is getting ready to retire. We need someone to create an event that will honor this person in an appropriate way.

Hint: It's possible—perhaps even likely—that none of these scenarios is a perfect fit for your sweet spot. That's okay. Have some fun as a group thinking about who would be best suited to each scenario, given the giftedness of everyone in the group. Isn't that actually the way it often is in life—that many times we don't have the "perfect" person for the job? In that case, who would be best to "fill in" until the ideal person shows up?

Here's another idea: if none of these scenarios fits you, try coming up with a scenario that would. Where and how might you make your best contribution?

FAQ

Q: Can a person have more than one sweet spot?

A: Not really. Sometimes it may seem as if someone can do almost anything. But close analysis will show that every person has a single core "sweet spot" that is unique to them. That sweet spot may fit them to do a relative handful of things well and with satisfaction, or it may fit them to do lots of different activities well and with satisfaction. It doesn't really matter how many activities fit one's sweet spot. A person has only one sweet spot.

In this light, consider that just because someone *can* do something doesn't mean they *love* to do it. There's a big difference between ability and *motivated* ability. In addition, just because someone enjoys doing an activity once or twice doesn't necessarily mean they want to do that thing over and over, all the time, from then on. Some sweet spots like to try something new just to learn it—and then move on.

We need to pay attention to the roles we prefer to play with other people. There's a reason why we prefer to be in charge, or to work in the background, or to take the initiative, or to collaborate with others, etc. That preference flows out of our sweet spots. Our relationships will benefit when we recognize and honor the legitimate roles we were designed by God to play, and we allow others to play the roles they were designed to play. In our relationships, as in the rest of our lives, we need to do most what we do best.

Sharing and Listening Activity 3

1. **Person 1:** Look back at Session Four, Sharing and Listening Activity 2, where you wrote a summary description of the best use of your gifts in a job.

2. In a similar way to what you did in Session Four concerning a job, how could you phrase your sweet spot description in terms of a volunteer ministry assignment?

Examples:

- "I would serve best in a volunteer position where I was working with children and materials to craft finished products and teach life lessons, following a structured program and clear instructions, and where I have a supervisor to call on when needed, in order to see kids gain confidence in their own skills and knowledge."

- "I would serve best in a situation where I could work with my hands on mechanical things—engines, motors, machines, equipment. I need time to figure out the problem and fix it, and I don't need supervision. Basically the satisfaction for me is to get things running again."

- "I can serve my church best by putting myself in situations that are highly political. I love to negotiate and make deals come together. So I can see myself working among the decision-makers to craft common understandings and work out plans that will be best for everyone concerned."

- "I love to come alongside people and help, especially in practical ways. I have a knack for handling money and budgets, so I could serve my church by helping people with money troubles, showing them how to set up a budget and stay within it. I'd need a guide or curriculum to follow, and it would help if I had a supervisor to turn to on an as-needed basis."

3. How does the description you just gave compare with any volunteer positions you are currently filling or have filled in the past?

When Person 1 is finished, turn the conversation around. Person 2 should now work through steps 1–3 above.

Pulling It Together

By now it should be clear that you are the same person with the same sweet spot whether you are at work, at home, at church, or anywhere. You bring your giftedness to everything you do. And the New Testament exhorts us to make our gifts available for service in the body of Christ.

Max Lucado said that when someone helped him identify his sweet spot, it enabled him to focus on what he does best. That's what we need to start doing—focusing our efforts on what we do best in our work, in our marriages, in our parenting, in our relationships, in our service to our church. In every area of our lives, we need to do most what we do best. Yes, there will always be areas of "can do" and "have to do" rather than "love to do." For that reason we need to live with servant's hearts. We must be willing at times to do the things that just need to be done, whether we're gifted to the task or not. But the main thrust of our lives should be our sweet spot. We should always look for ways to exercise our giftedness, as God gives us opportunity.

And there's one other thing we should do—we should keep telling stories about things we've enjoyed doing and done well. We can make that a life-long habit. Doing so immediately gets us in touch with our giftedness, and having an awareness of our giftedness is a powerful truth. It's the truth of how God has made us. He made each one of us the way we are, and he delights when we live who we are. Let's live our lives to his glory.

Lord, what a marvelous God you are! Psalm 8 reminds me that you have made all things—everything I see in the universe. And as I consider all the wonders of nature, I am awed and ask, "What are we as humans, so small and seemingly insignificant, that you would take notice of us?" And yet your Word says that we are your greatest creation, and that you have crowned us with glory and majesty. Oh, Lord, I have seen some of that glory and majesty in the stories I've told in this group. I've seen in simple but profound ways how you have gifted each one of us, and fitted us for a purpose. Lord, help me to find and follow that purpose. Help me to pay attention to my sweet spot. Help me to refine and deepen my understanding of my sweet spot. And help me to use my strengths for good—to carry out those "good works" that you prepared for me before you ever created me. Thank you, God, for handcrafting each one of us. My life begins and ends in you. May I bring you glory through the way I live this day and every day.

Learning to Pay Attention: A Lifelong Habit

Hopefully you've made a lot of new discoveries about yourself as you've participated in this *Cure for the Common Life Small Group Study*. And hopefully those discoveries have given you confidence to lay hold of your giftedness and exercise it to the glory of God and for the benefit of others. So would you like to continue that process throughout your life? This group has shown you a simple but powerful means for doing that. It involves paying attention as a lifelong habit.

Think back to when you first learned to drive a car. Remember how many things you had to pay attention to? Staying in your lane. Watching for stop signs and other traffic controls. Keeping the right distance behind other vehicles. Using your turn signal before making a turn. It seemed like there were a thousand things to remember, and you had to pay a *lot* of attention. But over time, most of those things became habits (hopefully). You began to do them automatically. They became "second nature," as they say.

Something similar needs to happen with your sweet spot. You need to develop a lifelong habit of paying attention to that sweet spot. Why? For the same reason that paying attention while driving has to become second nature: because of all the distractions. When you're driving, there are lots of things that try to pull your attention away from what's happening on the road. The music on the radio or CD player. Your kids laughing in the back seat. Your cell phone ringing. Roadside advertisements calling out to you. Lots of off-the-road stuff going on! Unless the habits of driving are second nature to you, you're liable to get distracted and—whoops!

So it is with your sweet spot. In this group you've paused to observe what your sweet spot is, and you've discovered that there really is a unique way in which you do live. But make no mistake, there are a thousand things that will try to distract you and get you out of your sweet spot. For instance: Advice that people give you that doesn't fit who you are. Feedback that isn't accurate to who you are. Requests or demands people make that don't fit you. Appeals for help in areas that don't fit your giftedness. There are countless ways in which you can get drawn out of your sweet spot. Unless you make it a habit to pay attention to that sweet spot, those distractions can tease you away from following your God-given design. And when that happens—you live ineffectively. You don't feel very good, either. You feel out of sorts. Because you *are* out of sorts. You're out of your sweet spot. You're not doing the thing that God designed you to do.

But that doesn't have to happen. By cultivating a lifelong habit of paying attention to your giftedness, you can put yourself on a continuous path of personal and spiritual growth, maturity, and effectiveness. This discussion group has already gotten you started on that path by taking you through a series of steps over and over. Now you can follow those same steps yourself. There are four steps to the process, as follows:

(1) Reflect

The first step in paying attention to yourself is to look back at something you did and ask, "What happened?" That's what you've been doing again and again by telling sweet spot stories and looking for patterns. That exercise has helped you go back to moments in your life when you were doing things that you enjoyed doing and felt you did well, and to pay attention to what you actually did. You reflected on what happened in order to see some things about yourself—perhaps things you'd never noticed before, even though they were right there for anyone to see, "hidden in plain sight."

(2) Connect

Once you've made some observations about what happened, you then need to ask, "What does it mean?" Again, this discussion group has provided you a process for understanding what your stories mean by giving you a framework for evaluating them. You looked for the five elements of S.T.O.R.Y. (Strengths, Topic, Optimal Conditions, Relationships, and Yes!). Those elements repeat in a pattern throughout your life, and by seeing that pattern, you begin to see that your life has a God-given design that fits you for certain situations and tasks.

(3) Project

Reflecting and Connecting are concerned with the past. The third step, Project, considers the future. Once you've learned some things about yourself by looking backwards, you're ready to look ahead into the future and ask, "What should I do because of this new learning?" In this group, you've been encouraged to "live into" your sweet spot—that is, to do most what you do best. That's appropriate advice as you look into your future, because God wants you to use the giftedness he gave you to do the "good works" that he intended for you (Eph. 2:10).

(4) Direct

The fourth step is the action step that asks, "What small, positive step can I take to act on what I have learned?" The group got you started on that step by helping you think about ways in which your sweet spot affects your work, your relationships, and your service at church. The point of this step is to *do* something as a result of the self-discovery you've made in the first three steps: Reflecting, Connecting, and Projecting. *Doing* something—even something small—is how you advance and make progress in your life. It's really a matter of "trust and obey." As God shows you new things about yourself, you can trust those new discoveries and then act on them, believing that God will work through the way he has made you to accomplish his purpose.

A Lifelong Habit

You will never go wrong by paying attention to your sweet spot. Your sweet spot is the way God designed you. So by Reflecting, Connecting, Projecting, and Directing, you are focusing on the core of what God intended when he made you. Nothing of consequence happens in your life apart from that core personhood. Everything that happens to you touches that core. Everything you do is affected by that core. The best of what you do flows from that core.

So pay attention to your sweet spot! You can do that anytime, anywhere, with almost anyone. You can always tell a sweet spot story—during dinner, while you're driving, while you're playing with your kids, when you're with some friends at the lake, when you run into someone at church, during a coffee break at work, on the phone with a friend. Talk about something you did that you enjoyed doing and feel you did well. Tell what happened. Examine what it means. Think about what it means for your future. Then determine what you'll do as a result of what you've learned.

If you will try that little exercise and start making it a habit in your life, you will experience a number of significant benefits, including:

- You will find yourself focusing on the positive.

- You will be in a better mood and feel better about yourself.

- You will discover more and more about your giftedness.

- You will start noticing other people's giftedness.

- You will meet with success as your God-given strengths make you more effective.

- You will gain more confidence.

- You will see God working through you.

- You will be a lot more grateful to God for what he has given you and what he is doing in and through you.

Enjoy the journey!

Facilitator's Guide

We want to thank you for taking the vital leadership role of facilitator in this *Cure for the Common Life Small Group Study*. Rather than invite group members to engage in a free-flowing discussion, this group will take participants through a very specific process aimed at a very intentional outcome—self-discovery. Your role as the facilitator is to help your group follow the process so that they experience the intended outcome.

The process is simple enough: Participants will tell certain stories from their lives about things they have done and enjoy doing and feel they do well. We call these "sweet spot stories," after the concept of the "sweet spot" developed by Max Lucado in *Cure for the Common Life* (see pages 1–8 in *Cure for the Common Life*). After telling their stories, participants will then examine those stories, looking for similar elements that show up in a recurring pattern. There are five things that make up that pattern, represented by the letters S.T.O.R.Y.:

S: What are your **Strengths**? What are the action words (or verbs) that you use to describe what you did? For example: "I planned," "I spoke," "I taught," "I built." We see your **Strengths** when you are in action.

T: What is your **Topic**? What are the things you work on, with, or through in your stories? For example: numbers, plants, machinery, money, a team, an audience, a concept, a language. We see your **Topic** in the things to which you apply **Strengths**.

O: What are your **Optimal Conditions**? What's the environment in which you thrive? For example: structure, crises, instructions, projects, potential, goals. We see your **Optimal Conditions** in the circumstances of your sweet spot.

R: What is your preferred **Relationship**? What relationship to others do you usually take on in your stories? Are you the person in charge, a follower, a collaborator, a team contributor, a Lone Ranger? We see your preferred **Relationship** in the role you like to play in your stories.

Y: What is your **Yes!**? What is the satisfaction you felt in your stories? What ultimate outcome gave you the most enjoyment? We see your **Yes!** in what made your activity seem worth doing.

This Discussion Group Is Different

So how does this small group study differ from the Sweet Spot Discovery Guide in *Cure for the Common Life* (found on pages 143–171)? The exercises in *Cure for the Common Life* are designed for individual readers to work through on their own, whereas this small group study is a group discussion and highly interactive. This small group study is intended to facilitate a *process*—the process of storytelling.

That means that this small group study is not a Bible study, nor is it a study guide for *Cure for the Common Life*. Again, this small group study facilitates a *process* of self-discovery. The underlying basis for this process is based on biblical principles, and the small group study will allude to numerous passages of Scripture, but it is not meant to take participants into an in-depth study of biblical texts. Likewise, the process is the same one that Max describes in *Cure for the Common Life*, and the small group study makes numerous references to material in *Cure for the Common Life*. But it does not ask participants to answer questions based on material in Max's book.

Why Your Group Needs You

That's the process—telling stories and looking for patterns. Sounds easy enough, right? It is, although most people need some help in order to tell their stories effectively, and then to spot patterns in those stories accurately. This is where you as the discussion facilitator can make all the difference. Your group will tell sweet spot stories in every session on this study, so be prepared to make the process as easy as possible for group members. Here are some elements to consider as you facilitate your group:

- **Make everyone comfortable.** Pick a meeting place that is suitable for breaking into twos and threes for conversation. Make sure everyone is introduced to each other and call people by their names during discussion times.

- **Start on time.** This is a matter of courtesy and respect. If your group needs some time to socialize before getting down to business, that's fine. Factor that in. But let people know the actual time when the discussion is going start. This group involves a sequential process that doesn't lend itself to people coming in late.

- **Keep the discussion on track.** This guide gives suggested times for the exercises the group will go through. Try to stay within those time frames. It's easy to get behind when people are telling stories. Exercise friendly but firm direction, if necessary, by calling out things like, "Let's take just two more minutes on this activity."

- **Keep it fun.** There is inherent fun in telling stories about the best moments of one's life, so the process itself should ensure a lively time. But you can help by fostering a positive, upbeat atmosphere. Smile, use humor, laugh, have a good time. This group is intended for celebration, not therapy.

- **Keep it positive.** The self-discovery in this group has to do with the giftedness that God has given to each participant. Giftedness is about one's strengths and what one does best. Don't allow group members to wander off on rabbit trails about each other's weaknesses, failures, or sins. Those are important matters, to be sure. But that's not the purpose of this group. Stick with the positives.

- **Respect people's boundaries.** The process of telling and examining "sweet spot stories" is inherently positive. Still, some participants may be guarded and unwilling to disclose. Respect their right to do that. Don't pry, and don't allow anyone in the group to bully others into revealing what they'd rather not talk about.

- **Watch for people who are struggling.** Some will have a hard time telling their stories. Others will struggle at looking for patterns. So pay attention to how all are doing as they go through the exercises. If you see someone looking hesitant, not participating, or in obvious distress, intervene and try to help. Make sure he understands the process, and ask him—privately, if necessary—how you can help.

- **Celebrate people's discoveries.** Participants *will* see new and exciting things about themselves through the course of this small group study, as well as confirm some previous discoveries about themselves. Either way, make a big deal out of those discoveries. They point to gifts that God designed into each person. Be a model for the group on how to honor God's workmanship by affirming other people's "sweet spots."

- **Make use of people's strengths.** One of the best ways to honor someone's "sweet spot" is to invite her to use her strengths in the group itself. For example, ask the person who is great at organizing to help you get things organized. Encourage the person who loves to facilitate understanding to spend extra time outside of the group with someone who doesn't quite "get" it. Challenge the person who likes to take charge to consider starting a small group of his own when your group is finished.

- **End on time.** As with starting on time, ending on time is a matter of courtesy and respect. The sessions in this small group study are designed to last about one to one and a half hours. Your group can last longer than that if it wants to, but you should set an expectation at the first meeting for how long the sessions will last, and then stick with that timeframe.

Make Sure You've Read the Book

It goes without saying that if you're going to facilitate a discussion group based on *Cure for the Common Life,* you should have read the book thoroughly at least once. Doing so will help you understand why the process in this small group study is needed and how it can be beneficial. In addition, it's inevitable that someone in the group will ask a question about something she's read in the book, or about something the book addresses. You'll be in a better position to help your group discuss that question if you have read the book.

Tailor the Process to Your Group

As you prepare to lead your group through this small group study, consider ways to tailor the process to your particular group. Small groups vary widely in terms of how well group members know each other, the purpose for which the group meets, the educational and socio-economic levels of participants, and many other factors. Think about what will work best for your group.

This small group study has been designed to offer a simple, basic process of telling stories and looking for patterns, and then applying people's self-discoveries to practical areas of their lives. However, you'll find material throughout that augments the basic process. Feel free to work that extra material into the discussion if you feel your group would benefit. But don't feel like you have to take your group through it.

Above All, Stick to the Process!

Whatever you do, stick with the basic process laid out in this guide. It has five decades of use to validate that it works. The only time it doesn't work is when people don't follow the process—when they add their own ideas about how to make it "work," or when they shortchange the process by not trusting it. You can trust it! PMI has been doing this process for fifty years. It works. Telling stories and looking for patterns really does yield tremendous insight.

What Should You Expect?

So if you follow the process, what should you as a leader expect to see?

- **Smiles and laughter.** Participants instinctively smile when they talk about the best moments of their lives. Some stories will summon up humorous memories and a good laugh, which is a healthy response.

- **Recognition and surprise.** Participants will begin to see themselves in their stories. Many will have core strengths confirmed that they've always known about, but perhaps haven't really recognized. Many participants will see new, positive things about themselves that they weren't aware of.

- **Tears and gratitude.** Some participants will be moved to tears of joy as they realize the value of what God has given them in their sweet spots. Joy will give way to gratitude as participants affirm their gifts and realize that what they do best is something God has always desired for them.

- **Praise.** Participants will be moved to thank and praise God for his good gifts—not only their own gifts, but the gifts of others.

- **Confidence.** Participants will take on a new confidence as they own their gifts and "live into" them, exercising their strengths at work, in their homes, and in the community of faith.

- **Connections.** Participants will start to see all kinds of connections between their sweet spot and what they do every day as a worker, a friend, a spouse, a parent, a member of the church, and a follower of Christ.

Pray for Your Group

We expect great things from this process! We've seen it do great things in the lives of tens of thousands of people. But there's something we urge you as a leader to do as a vital preparation for the process: *pray for your group*. If you already know their names, pray for them specifically by name. As you pray, ask God to:

- Help the group work well together. There is great power in a small group of God's people, especially when they gather to seek God's truth. Ask God to be present among his people, and to do his work in and among the members of the group.

- Help them to discover, own, and celebrate their gifts. Self-discovery is one of the primary purposes of the group. So ask God to carry out that purpose by providing insight into everyone's giftedness.

- Help them see God's hand in their life histories. Just as God's people have always remembered how he has intervened at key moments in their histories, so the stories told in this group will show God's handiwork in the lives of the group members. Ask God to help participants see how much he has delighted in the expression of their gifts throughout their lives.

- Help them gain hope for what their lives can be. Everyone needs hope. By grasping the significance of the gifts they've been given, participants can look forward to more meaningful, purposeful lives as they look for ways to stay in their sweet spots.

- Help them live into their giftedness. God gave us our gifts for a reason: He wants us to use them to make a contribution to his kingdom and to the world. Ask God to help group members act on what they learn about themselves in every area of their lives.

A Special Note about Session One

As written, Session One is an introductory session designed for a group that is just getting started in the sweet spot discovery process. It assumes that group participants are coming to the group for the first time, with no preparation ahead of time. One of the things they are asked to do (in Activity 3) is to recall stories from their lives about things they did that they enjoyed doing and feel they did well. At the end of the session they are asked to make an actual list of such "sweet spot activities" prior to Session Two.

You can accelerate the progress of your group by having participants come to Session One having already made a list of 8–10 sweet spot activities. If you do that, you will likely have time to tell an additional story, using the guidelines given in Activity 3 of Session One. The more stories your group is able to tell during Sessions One, Two, and Three, the better. It means you'll have more to work with as you to try to figure out the S.T.O.R.Y. elements that make up people's sweet spots.

If you want your group to prepare a list of sweet spot activities ahead of time, send them a letter or e-mail that provides instructions for doing that. Here's a sample letter:

Dear Group Member,

I hope you are looking forward to the first meeting of our Cure for the Common Life *discussion group! We will meet at [TIME] on [DATE] at [LOCATION].*

In order to make the best use of our time at that initial meeting, I want to ask you to come up with a list of what are called "sweet spot activities." In Cure for the Common Life, *Max Lucado explains that a sweet spot is the place on a golf club or baseball bat or tennis racket that delivers the most power and control out of one's swing. People have sweet spots, too. The way to find yours is to look at times in your life when you were doing an activity you enjoyed doing and felt you did it well.*

That's what we're going to do in our Cure for the Common Life *discussion group. But in preparation for our first meeting, we'll need for you to prepare a list of sweet spot activities.*

Here are examples of the kind of activities we are looking for:

- *As a child I read a list of books in order to win a prize.*

- *As a child I caught the final out in a softball game, and our team won.*

- *In junior high school I tap danced in a talent show.*

- *In junior high school I started learning to play the viola, and by the end of a year I was first chair in the school orchestra.*

- *In high school I went to camp and learned to water ski.*

- *In high school I had a summer job as a swim instructor, and became the head instructor over kids who were older than me.*

- *As a young adult I passed a certification exam on the first try—one of only two people out of thirty to pass the exam. And I had the flu the day I took it!*

- *As a college student I planned a trip to Europe for me and three of my friends. I budgeted so well that we came back with extra money.*

- *As an adult I made a presentation at work that caused my company to change strategies and ultimately earned me a promotion.*

- *As an adult I helped my aging parents think through their assisted living plans and got them into a good facility.*

Come up with your own list of sweet spot activities. The two criteria for determining whether an activity should go on the list are:

(1) Was it an activity you enjoyed doing? Did you find satisfaction in doing it?

(2) Did you accomplish something? That is, did you do something to make the activity happen, as opposed to just having an experience?

If possible, come up with at least a dozen activities from throughout your life that satisfy those two criteria.

Thanks for doing this, and I look forward to seeing you at our first meeting!

Session One—What's Your Story?

If this session is serving as your introductory session, make sure that the participants are introduced to one another. If the participants have not yet read the Introduction, you might want to encourage them to spend a few minutes reading it to themselves, or read aloud selected passages that illustrate the overall goal of this small group study.

Getting Started

Have someone read this section aloud.

Sharing and Listening Activity 1 (5 minutes)

Allow five minutes for this activity. Be ready to step in and assign partners if the group seems to be uncomfortable pairing off themselves. Partners should change with each session so that the participants can get as many different perspectives on their stories as possible.

Paying Attention

Have someone read this section aloud.

Sharing and Listening Activity 2 (5–7 minutes)

Before beginning this activity, you might want to have the group read through the sidebars "What Do We Mean by Satisfaction?" and "What's the Satisfaction?" for additional guidance.

Motivate Me! (10–15 minutes)

Read the following questions aloud, allowing a few group members to respond after each question:

(1) Did anyone hear something from the person next to you that caused you to say, "I knew she was going to say that!" How did you know she would talk about that activity?

(2) Did anyone learn something about the person next to you that you had never known before? Tell us what you heard.

Then have someone read the text of this section aloud.

Sharing and Listening Activity 3 (10 minutes)

Before beginning this activity, refer the group to the examples in the sidebar "Things I Enjoyed Doing and Did Well."

Reflecting (20–25 minutes)

Read the following questions aloud, allowing a few group members to respond after each question:

(1) If the only thing you knew about the person next to you was the story she just told, what would be your guess as to what she is

motivated to do? In other words, what would you say she likes to do, and how does she go about doing it?

(2) The person next to you told about something he really enjoyed doing. What was the satisfaction he took from that activity? How could you tell he enjoyed it?

(3) How does the activity that the person next to you just told you about compare with the activity she told you about before? Any similarities?

(4) How many of you told a story that you have never told anyone before? How did it feel to tell the person next to you about what you did when you were in your sweet spot, and what you found so satisfying about it?

Then have someone read the text of this section aloud.

Pulling It Together

Have someone read the following section aloud.

For the Next Session

Encourage participants to do the following:

(1) Tell a trusted friend or loved one about the satisfying activities you described in this session. Be sure to describe what it is about those activities that feels so satisfying.

(2) Using the guide provided here, make a list of activities you have done in your life that you enjoyed doing and feel you did well. Put as many items on the list as you like. The key is that you found the activities satisfying.

Close the session in prayer.

Session Two—Unpack Your Life

Getting Started
Have someone read this section aloud.

Sharing and Listening Activity 1 (10 minutes)
Allow five minutes for each person to share. Refer the participants to the sidebar "What Was So Satisfying?" for more insight.

Reflecting (10–15 minutes)
Read the following question aloud, allowing a few group members to respond:

Did anyone learn something about the person next to you that you had never known before? Tell us what you heard. What was the satisfaction that the person next to you gained from the activity he described? As you listened to the person next to you tell his story, what action words (or verbs) did you hear him use to describe what he did?

Allow a few minutes for each person to journal on the additional questions in the section.

Sharing and Listening Activity 2 (10 minutes)
Allow five minutes for each person to share.

Focusing (10–15 minutes)
Read the following question aloud, allowing a few group members to respond:

What was the satisfaction that the person next to you gained from the activity she just described? As you listened to the person next to you tell her story, what action words (or verbs) did you hear her use to describe what she did?

Allow a few minutes for each person to journal on the additional questions in the section.

Sharing and Listening Activity 3 (10 minutes)
Allow five minutes for each person to share.

Discovering (10–15 minutes)
Read the following question aloud, allowing a few group members to respond:

> *What was the satisfaction that the person next to you gained from the activity he just described? As you listened to the person next to you tell his story, what action words (or verbs) did you hear him use to describe what he did? Did anyone notice any similarities between the three stories that you have heard from the person next to you in this session? Describe those similarities.*

Allow a few minutes for each person to journal on the additional questions in the section.

Allow an additional few minutes for the last element in this section:

> *By listening to the person next to you tell her stories, you've now seen three snapshots of that person when she was in her sweet spot. Take a moment to tell the person next to you what you see her doing when she is in her sweet spot.*

Pulling It Together
Have someone read the text of this section aloud.

For the Next Session
Encourage participants to do the following:

(1) If you haven't already done so, make a list of activities you have done in your life that you enjoyed doing and feel you did well. Put as many items on the list as you like. The key is that you found the activities satisfying. (Use the guide provided on page 8).

(2) Review the activities you talked about in Session One and Session Two.

- Can you see any similarities between them?

- Are there any common themes about the satisfaction you take from your sweet spot activities?

- Are there any action words (verbs) that keep repeating in your stories?

(3) Your design has significant implications for your everyday life. So think about the five areas of life listed below. Put a star next to the area(s) where knowing your design could be the most helpful in your life. Perhaps it's the area in which you are currently experiencing the greatest frustrations.

_____ Work

_____ Marriage

_____ Parenting

_____ Relationships

_____ Involvement in church

Close the session in prayer.

Session Three—Study Your S.T.O.R.Y.

Getting Started

Welcome your group back and ask them a few questions:

Has anyone noticed his sweet spot showing up at work or at home or somewhere else? For instance, did people comment on something you did that, to you, seemed like nothing, but to them seemed quite remarkable? Or did you get so involved in an activity that you lost track of time?

Allow time for group members to respond.
Then have someone read the text of this section aloud.

Sharing and Listening Activity 1 (10 minutes)

Encourage participants to find a different partner than they've had in previous sessions. Allow five minutes per person to share.

Reflecting (10–15 minutes)

Read the following question aloud, allowing a few group members to respond:

What was the satisfaction that the person next to you gained from the activity she described? As you listened to the person next to you tell her story, what action words (or verbs) did you hear her use to describe what she did?

Allow a few minutes for each person to journal on the additional questions in the section.

Sharing and Listening Activity 2 (10 minutes)

Allow five minutes for each person to share.

Focusing (10-15 minutes)

Read the following question aloud, allowing a few group members to respond:

What was the satisfaction that the person next to you gained from the activity he just described? As you listened to the person next to you tell his story, what action words (or verbs) did you hear him use to describe what he did?

Allow a few minutes for each person to journal on questions 1-3 in this section.

Sharing and Listening Activity 3 (10 minutes)

Allow five minutes for each person to share.

Discovering (10–15 minutes)

Read the following question aloud, allowing a few group members to respond:

What was the satisfaction that the person next to you gained from the activity she just described? As you listened to the person next to you tell her story, what action words (or verbs) did you hear her use to describe what she did?

Allow a few minutes for each person to journal on the additional questions in the section.

Allow an additional few minutes for the last element in this section:

• By listening to the person next to you tell his stories, you've now seen three snapshots of that person when he was in his sweet spot. Take a moment to tell the person next to you what you see him doing when he is in his sweet spot.

Pulling It Together

Have someone read the text of this section aloud.

For the Next Session

Encourage participants to do the following:

(1) Review the sweet spot activities you talked about in the first three sessions of the group. If you'd like, find an objective partner to help you examine your stories and look for patterns in them.

- What similarities do you see among your stories?

- What activities do you keep coming back to again and again?

- Are there any action words (verbs) that keep repeating in your stories?

- Is there a particular role that you enjoy playing in your stories (for example: advisor, helper, cheerleader, idea originator, problem solver, etc.)?

- Are there any common themes about the satisfaction you take from your sweet spot activities?

Close the session in prayer.

Session Four—Take Your Job and Love It

Getting Started

Have someone read this section aloud.

Sharing and Listening Activity 1 (30 minutes)

Allow ten minutes for each person to share. Be available to assist in case the groups have questions on identifying action words.

Note: If not everyone can be divided into sub-groups of three, some people should pair up into twos. For example, a group of eight should divide into two sub-groups of three and one sub-group of two.

Note: If you have members of your group who work together, discourage them being members of the same trio. There are potential political repercussions involved in people talking openly about a poor job fit in front of supervisors, coworkers, customers, vendors, etc.

Working Matters

Have someone read this section aloud.

Sharing and Listening Activity 2 (15 minutes)

Have participants spend five minutes journaling in response to questions 1-4 and then spend ten minutes sharing their thoughts with their group of three. Point out the various sidebars that may be helpful during this time.

Creating a Better Fit

Have someone read this section aloud.

Sharing and Listening Activity 3 (15 minutes)

Have participants work through questions 1–3 for each person in the group.

Pulling It Together

Have someone read this section aloud.

For the Next Session

Encourage participants to do the following:

(1) Review your description of your "what I do best" job. Go back to your stories and what you learned about yourself from them and see if you can refine that description into a clear statement of the job you would do best.

(2) Show your refined description of your "what I do best" job to someone who knows you well. Discuss the implications of that description for your current job, as well as for your future jobs.

(3) Talk with that same person about the strategy you could use to make the best of your less-than-ideal job-fit. How can you get started on implementing that strategy right away?

Close the session in prayer.

Session Five—Discover Your Role

Getting Started

Have someone read this section aloud.

Sharing and Listening Activity 1 (20 minutes)

Allow ten minutes for each person to share.

Expanding Our Views

Have someone read this section aloud.

Sharing and Listening Activity 2 (20 minutes)

Allow ten minutes for each person to share.

At the end of Activity 2, transition into Activity 3 as follows:

We've been examining our stories to see how we tend to relate to people when we are in our sweet spots. Would some of you volunteer to talk about what roles you prefer to play in your stories?

(Allow as many group members as would like to describe their preferred roles. As they do, ask if others in the group can give examples of when they have seen each other playing their preferred roles.)

After completing a few minutes of group sharing, read the following aloud:

As we relate to other people, Scripture tells us to 'encourage one another, and build each other up' (1 Thess. 5:11 NIV). Yet our tendency when we encounter others who see and do things differently than we do is to think (or say), "What's wrong with you?" But now that we know about sweet spots, we can see that there's nothing wrong with others for being different than we are. The truth is, God has made each person to be unique, and each of us is living out our uniqueness.

Let's go back to the people we were talking with in the previous activity and look more closely at how our sweet spots affect our relationships.

Sharing and Listening Activity 3 (10 minutes)
Allow ten minutes for each person to share.

Reflecting
Have someone read this section aloud.

Sharing and Listening Activity 4 (10 minutes)
Allow five minutes for each person to share.

Pulling It Together
Have someone read this section aloud.

For the Next Session
Encourage participants to do the following:

(1) Talk with someone who knows you well—your spouse, a friend, a family member—about what your stories reveal about the way you prefer to relate to others.

(2) Reflect on the key relationships you currently have in your life. How does your sweet spot affect those relationships—for better or for worse? How can you build those relationships without changing who you are?

Close the session in prayer.

Session Six—Be the Body

Getting Started
Have someone read this section aloud.

Sharing and Listening Activity 1 (20 minutes)
Allow ten minutes for each person to share and reflect.

Focusing
Have someone read this section aloud.

Sharing and Listening Activity 2 (15 minutes)
Allow approximately seven minutes for each person to share.

Considering Your Strengths

Read the following question aloud, allowing a few group members to respond:

Would someone volunteer to tell us what ideas you came up with for roles that you could play in the work of the church?

(Allow as many group members as would like to describe their roles aloud.) Read the following aloud, allowing group members to respond as follows:

Let's follow up this discussion with an activity about situations that we might find at a church. As I read each of the scenarios below, think about what kind of person is needed for the situation. If it sounds like your sweet spot is called for, speak up and tell us why you fit the situation. Also tell us what the phrase or slogan for your sweet spot role is.

Hint: It's possible—perhaps even likely—that none of these scenarios is a *perfect* fit for your sweet spot. That's okay. Have some fun as a group thinking about who would be *best* suited to each scenario, given the giftedness of everyone in the group. Isn't that actually the way it often is in life—that many times we don't have the "perfect" person for the job? In that case, who would be best to "fill in" until the ideal person shows up?

Here's another idea: if none of these scenarios fits you, try coming up with a scenario that *would* fit you. Where and how might you make your *best* contribution?

Scenarios:

(1) We need someone to get an office organized—papers filed, equipment set up properly, contents of drawers put in order, things labeled accurately, and so on.

(2) An emergency strikes. We need someone with a clear head to assess the situation, formulate a plan for response, mobilize people, and get things under control.

(3) A neighbor is going through a divorce. She is past the shock of it, but feels like she needs someone to talk to. We need someone who can listen and respond calmly and wisely to what she has to say.

(4) A youth group from the church is going on a mission trip to help rebuild a church that was damaged in a hurricane. We need someone to go as an assistant to the youth leaders and help keep the kids on task.

(5) We need someone to figure out what has broken down on an old bus and, if possible, get it running again.

(6) A group of men in the church have organized a softball team and joined a league. They need someone to coach the team.

(7) The women's ministry is getting ready to hold a conference. We need someone to put together a notebook for the conference attendees that will hold all of their notes, presentation slides, and additional information for the conference.

(8) A longtime leader of a civic organization is getting ready to retire. We need someone to create an event that will honor this person in an appropriate way.

Sharing and Listening Activity 3 (10 minutes)

Allow five minutes for each person to share.

Pulling It Together

Take a few minutes to walk through this activity:

> *We've just taken a few minutes to refine our descriptions of our sweet spots into statements of what our ideal volunteer ministry positions would look like. We've gotten to know each other pretty well through these six sessions. So as we start to bring this group to a close, let's go around the group and have each person read the description they just came up with.*

(Allow each group member to read his description.)

When all are finished reading their descriptions, have someone read the text in this section aloud.

If you wish, spend some time in group prayer, allowing everyone to thank God for their own giftedness and/or for the giftedness of others in the group.

Learn to Pay Attention

This section is extremely important to share with your group. Take turns reading the entire section aloud during your last session or ask participants to read it aloud in their small groups. Use the method that best fits your group, but be sure to allot some time to go through this section with them.

About People Management International, Inc.

People Management International, Inc. (PMI) is an international consulting firm with offices in the United States, Europe, and Australia. Since 1961, PMI has served both corporate and not-for-profit organizations, as well as individuals, through executive search, executive coaching, organizational effectiveness, and assessment. All of PMI's work is based on its proprietary assessment technology, the System for Identifying Motivated Abilities (SIMA®).

SIMA® has been used to identify giftedness for hundreds of thousands of individuals, and to apply that understanding in strategic people management at hundreds of organizations in a wide variety of fields. SIMA® is a very powerful tool for pinpointing the uniqueness of an individual in a positive, comprehensive, and non-psychological way when used by a trained, licensed practitioner who is a certified member of PMI.

However, in order to make SIMA® available on a wider basis, PMI has licensed certain groups and individuals to distribute derivative (i.e. simpler and less technical) versions of SIMA®. Max Lucado and Thomas Nelson, Inc. were allowed to develop the S.T.O.R.Y. approach for *Cure for the Common Life* and this companion small group study. That means that S.T.O.R.Y. is based on a proven methodology that promises real results when followed properly. It also means that S.T.O.R.Y. is proprietary and should be used only in connection with *Cure for the Common Life* and *Cure for the Common Life Small Group Study*.

If you or your organization has needs that go beyond the scope and intent of S.T.O.R.Y., or if you would like to find out more about PMI's wide range of products and services for both individuals and organizations, contact PMI at the website below. PMI has offices throughout the United States, with specialists in career guidance, as well as consultants with expertise in every aspect of human resources and strategic people management. Contact us at:

People Management International, Inc.
P.O. Box 1004
Avon, Connecticut 06001-1004
Email: info@peoplemanagement.org
On the web: www.peoplemanagement.org

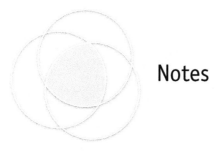

Notes

Notes

Notes

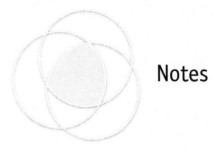

Notes

Notes

Notes

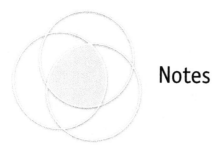

Notes

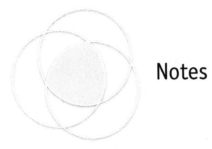

Notes

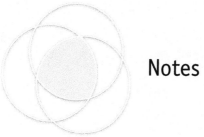

Notes

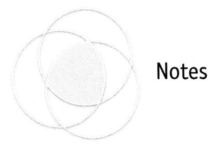

Notes

Lucado Life Lesson Series

The Gospel of Mark
1-4185-0942-6

The Gospel of Luke
1-4185-0943-4

The Gospel of John
1-4185-0944-2

Acts
1-4185-0945-0

Romans
1-4185-0946-9

1 Corinthians
1-4185-0947-7

Revised and updated, the Lucado Life Lessons series is perfect for small group or individual use and includes intriguing questions that will take you deeper into God's Word.

THOMAS NELSON
Since 1798

Available at your local Christian Bookstore

Cure for the
Common Life

▸ Available in Spanish

MAX LUCADO

Autor del éxitos de librería según el *New York Times*

Cura para la vida común

Encontrando SU lugar.

CARIBE-BETANIA EDITORES
Una división de Thomas Nelson Publishers

www.caribebetania.com

ISBN: 084990008S